CW01082263

LOOK AT ME:
Celebrating the Self in
Modern Britain

LOOK AT ME:
Celebrating the Self in
Modern Britain

By
Peter Whittle

Carol –
All the best + thanks for
all your great support!

love
Peter –

British Library Cataloguing in Publication Data
A catalogue record of this book is available from the British Library

Printed and bound in the United Kingdom

ISBN 978-1-904863-31-1

Social Affairs Unit
314–322 Regent Street
London W1B 5SA
www.socialaffairsunit.org.uk

CONTENTS

For my parents,
Joan and Peter, who never said it

ACKNOWLEDGEMENTS

I would like to express my gratitude to Michael Mosbacher, director of the Social Affairs Unit, first for his enthusiasm when I initially went to him with the idea for this book, and then for his patience when I repeatedly stretched the deadline. I would also like to thank my excellent editor Clive Liddiard, who, perhaps mindful that this was my first time, was very gentle.

CHAPTER ONE

WAX ROLE MODELS

> Fame is like a river, that beareth up things light and
> swollen, and drowns things weighty and solid.
>
> Francis Bacon

One of my most vivid memories of a Sixties London
childhood was being taken by my parents to Madame
Tussauds. Tickets were expensive – there were four of us and
money was tight. This year, instead of a holiday away, we
were going out 'for days'. At the end of our tour, we squeezed
into a tiny recording booth in the foyer and produced a
45 rpm record as a souvenir of our visit.

'Now,' says my mother hesitantly on the crackly sound-
track, 'who have you seen today? You've seen the Queen,
haven't you?'

'Yes', says a squeaky little high-pitched voice.

'And the Beatles?'

'We saw the Beatles', echoes my sister's even higher, even
squeakier voice.

'And there were the astronaut men, weren't there?'
I remember us just nodding at this point. 'And there was
Nelson on his ship, wasn't there, with his one eye?'

'Hmm.'

'Shall we sing a song, then?' asks my father. 'Come on...'

Eng-er-land swings like a pendulum do,

Mummy's gonna buy you a two-by-two,

Westminster Abbey, the Tower, Big Ben,

The rosy red cheeks of the little child-ren...

The experience of Tussauds was one of the most exciting I had ever had. I couldn't get it out of my head for weeks. Those wax models had set my imagination firing. It was big and grand and dramatic. I can honestly say that what was to become a childhood interest with history, and even art, started in those rooms on Baker Street.

There was Mary, Queen of Scots at the point of execution. There was Louis XVI and Marie Antoinette, modelled in their finery as they would have appeared before the deluge. Misty with dry ice, HMS *Victory* creaked and moaned as Nelson succumbed below deck. *And When Did You Last See Your Father?* – that famous Victorian painting of the son of a Cavalier being questioned by Roundheads – was brought to life, of a sort. On a raised single plinth, complete with sun hat and cigar, Churchill sat and contemplated the canvas in front of him.

The tableaux and figures were cordoned off behind ropes, and the dense crowds moved slowly from one exhibit to the next. A large group of literary figures, among them Dickens, Byron and Sir Walter Scott, stared out of a library setting. Sinatra sat in the middle of a massive champagne glass, which emitted bubbles. Under a huge bell jar, Rudolf Nureyev practised in front of a mirror, as psychedelic lights flashed and pop music came in bursts – this was the Swinging Sixties after all. At the centre of the main hall stood the Royals – the whole extended family that is, right down to the Duchess of Kent. On one side was a row of American presidents, on the other the British Cabinet and Opposition. Tussauds then had a quasi-museum status, and it was all strictly look but don't touch. Not that one wanted to – it all had a far-off, glamorous aura, especially to my young eyes; and it was, in its way, utterly inspiring.

I went back as a teenager, and later with young nieces and nephews. Henry Moore, Agatha Christie and Audrey Hepburn, in full Eliza Dolittle rig, came and went. Branwell Brontë painted his sisters at one point. Marat, modelled after the painting by David, remained as ever, murdered in his bath by Charlotte Corday. But in the intervening years, the models gradually lost their plinths and became more accessible, as the principle of 'visitor-friendliness', now so beloved of all public attractions, was increasingly embraced. Then, at some point, the historical tableaux disappeared, as did the famous queue outside the building, as the ticketing halls were redesigned. When new figures were unveiled to the media, the publicity would crow about how one could now squeeze Brad Pitt's backside, kiss Jennifer Lopez on the cheek and canoodle with Prince William. And then, in 2007, Tussauds excitedly announced that, for a hefty fee of £150,000, obscurity would no longer be a bar, and you too could be immortalised in wax for exhibition – presumably in your own living room. Why anyone would want to do this was a complete mystery to me; I thought it might be a good time for a return visit.

It didn't take long for it to become clear that the place, which had once been something of an institution, had become a 3D version of *Hello!* magazine. From the moment one stepped out of the lift to be confronted by the fake sounds and sight of a row of paparazzi, it was clear that Tussauds had given itself up wholesale to the supposed universal fascination with the cult of celebrity. A few months previously, it had been reported, with a few murmurings of regret, that the Planetarium next door had finally thrown in the towel and been replaced by an animated show, inviting people to step into the 'wonderful world of stars'. Madame Tussauds had clearly been similarly inspired, except that its 'stars' were of a more down-to-earth variety. The exhibition itself had jettisoned any pretensions to gravitas it might once have had, and was a celebration of fame pure and simple. It was disposable, hollow, and thoroughly tin-pot.

Stars had always been on show, of course; but they had been just part of it. Popular familiarity was obviously now the guiding principle, and the great and the good took their places, regardless of relative distinction, in this strict pecking order, from Kylie Minogue down. There was a likeness of just one writer in the whole collection (Dickens, inevitably). Otherwise, the arts were represented by two figures – Van Gogh and Shakespeare – squeezed up against Einstein in an unpopulated, un-photographed corner. Perennial favourites like Victoria, Henry VIII and Elizabeth remained, but most of the British monarchs had gone, as had the majority of past prime ministers, and all contemporary British politicians except Blair. David Cameron – who once would have been an immediate fixture as leader of the Opposition – was obviously not deemed worthy. The Royal family had been severely trimmed back, the Queen losing three of her children to the melting vat. The astronauts were still there – no longer in their moon setting, but stuck behind Gandhi and the Dalai Lama: a cluster presumably meant to represent someone's idea of New Age spirituality.

All ropes and restraint had gone, and the gawping crowds were now positively encouraged to drape themselves over the models, which they did indiscriminately at every opportunity. As tourism management jargon would have it, the visitor was now firmly 'at the centre of the experience' – literally, with queues of them awaiting their chance to address a fake UN press conference ('The World Awaits!') flanked by Bush and Blair, or gurn at the camera with arms slung around HM's shoulders, or cuddle up to Robbie Williams mid-performance. The crowds seemed to want, more than anything, to have their pictures taken with someone – anyone – famous, almost regardless of what they were famous for, and possibly in the hope that some celebrity-dust would rub off. All this grinning, gesticulating and posing for the benefit of phone-snapping friends made a clear view of any of the portraits impossible. The effect was like being force-fed the stag-party photos of a thousand strangers, and it was a relief to emerge into daylight after barely an hour.

The simple experience of touring this collection of effigies and watching the public reaction to them was interesting in the way it reflected some of the profound changes that have swept through society over the past 40 years. The death of unthinking deference might be no bad thing; but its place has been taken by an equally blind lack of discrimination. One sensed that, for many visitors, most of the likenesses on show were of people who were members of a single class, The

Famous, and the talent, position and distinction (or complete lack of all three) that might have put them there came a poor second. They were simply part of a growing sector of society that had achieved what we might call High Visibility Status. They were special – something that everybody could, and should, aspire to. Consequently, the attitude of the visitors hogging everybody else's sightlines was not one of admiration and collective recognition; rather, they evinced a kind of *ownership* of these familiar faces, which was expressed through a mateyness laced with an underlying envy and contempt. And the thoughts of others looking on counted for nothing.

It was easier to understand after this why Tussauds might think there was a market for their model-making services among otherwise obscure, paying customers (though most of the people there on that day would probably have balked at the fee). The place attracts millions through its doors, as it always has, but what it now seems to provide is a huge mirror in which the public can view its own face. My childhood visit to Madame Tussauds led me, in a roundabout but oddly logical way, to the National Portrait Gallery; but it was hard to see what today's kids could have got out of their visit, other than the quick thrill of a fairground attraction, and the belief that to be recognisable to others – in whatever shape or form, and by whatever means – is the ultimate goal. And if this means making an utter fool of yourself, then no matter: it will be worth it.

In today's media, it is a truism (albeit a highly debatable one) that the presence of a celebrity is crucial in drawing the public's attention to a new book, film, play or TV show. So, in that spirit, we should explore this – the sharper, cutting end of the search for Specialness – before we look at the wider picture and what has brought us to this pass. In setting the scene, however, it is worth pondering why it should be that, with so many A-, B- and Z-list names now clogging up the pages and airwaves, it remains a constantly heard complaint that there are no heroes anymore, no real stars (as we might once have understood the term), and nobody to lift the spirits, inspire us, or make us feel as one.

'I think being famous has become rather common, actually', said the actor Rupert Everett, with his trademark hauteur, in a recent *Spectator* article. 'I don't really respect the sort of people who get to be famous these days. That whole world doesn't seem at all glamorous any more – the films aren't glamorous, the music isn't and the people you see getting out of the private jets aren't. I think there is something rather tragic about it, actually.'

Perhaps Gilbert and Sullivan got it right a century ago, when they wrote in *The Gondoliers*:

When everybody's somebody,
Then no one's anybody!

CHAPTER TWO

SELF-DRAMATIS PERSONAE

Say 'Hiya' to Kayleigh. Kayleigh is recovering after a wicked night out with her mates, during which they'd driven around the West End of London in a White Stretch Limo that they'd all banded together to hire. It was totally cool, watching people on the pavement squinting to see who might be inside. Of course, Kayleigh and her friends hadn't bargained for the celebrity-protecting dark windows, and with a slight flicker of panic had realised that the point of their jaunt might be rendered void. So, one by one, up they'd got onto the seats, emerging crop-topped through the sun-roof into the traffic-filled, neon-lit street. Indignant at the unimpressed expressions of passers-by, Kayleigh had felt aggrieved, and had taken to shouting 'Jealous!' at anybody who failed to smile. Most people had just hurried on, the boring bastards. Still, at least they'd noticed her.

Nobody's going to hold Kayleigh back. She's only 18, but she knows she's going to be famous – and soon. Nothing's going to get in her way, and she won't take any crap from anyone trying to tell her otherwise. Ashley, her boyfriend, tells her respect is everything. She deserves respect, is what Ashley says. Her teachers didn't respect her; they tried to get round her just so she'd do the things they wanted her to do. They were, like, so stupid.

Her mum and dad always knew she was special, always wanted to be the centre of attention, and so always encouraged her – which was good, because that way she'd get to express her personality. She's already saving up for a boob job. Nan doesn't like this and wishes she'd change her mind; but as

Kayleigh says, 'I'm not doing this for anyone else; I'm doing this for me.' She heard that line on *Trisha*, and she repeats it whenever one of her snobbier mates 'as a go at her about it.

* * * * *

Meet Harriet. Twenty-eight and single, she lives in one of the shabbier parts of Central London, and works for a public relations company specialising in event management. She is, essentially, a party planner for corporate clients, although she refers to herself as a 'producer'.

Harriet *totally* loves her job, which allows her to give full rein to the unique creative insights she always knew she possessed. She is averagely pretty and has her fair share of dates, although nobody has yet ticked all her boxes. The romantic game feels increasingly like a round of auditions, with her mentally sitting back, feet up on the table, cigar between finger and thumb, judging the calibre of the latest applicant. It's starting to get just a bit exhausting. Still, there's no hurry, and she so has no intention of compromising. She deserves the best, and she knows she's worth it.

Harriet eats out most nights. When friends do come round, she makes a big display of her empty fridge, pointing with mock horror at the pot noodles past their sell-by date and the half-empty bottle of champagne. 'I'm *so* sad', she exclaims, knowing, of course, that they would have clocked how in demand she is. Her three best friends all think she's right not to settle on the man-front. They have a good time anyway, the four of them, going out on the town, living their own, less expensively dressed version of *Sex and the City*, a show that they all think is *totally* amazing and which they completely identify with. They are, in fact, a pretty amazing quartet themselves: sometimes they laugh and shout each other hoarse; sometimes they get smashed. Occasionally they end up with an old fart at the next table who complains about the noise. Harriet thinks this is totally bizarre behaviour; people should just go off and get a life.

Harriet loves coming home to her one-bedroom flat. It's her retreat from the world, and she can do what she likes, and she can spoil herself rotten. She's been in this place for six years, but knows little about the area. What's it got to do with her? She's not friends with anyone else in the building; she doesn't do neighbours.

* * * * *

Marc is white hot in marketing. In fact, he won Personality of the Year at the Marketing Awards last year. The problem is he can't find anywhere appropriate to display the somewhat gaudy bauble in the immaculately interior-decorated minimalist apartment which he shares with his partner, Sue. The shiny floorboards, stark white walls and few pieces of agonisingly tasteful furniture are a set for the two of them to exist on, the controlled starkness of the background throwing their personalities and nonchalantly glamorous figures into sharp relief. In the end, they bow to tradition with a giggle and decide to put the award in full view on the mantelpiece, where it can be enjoyed ironically by their friends. Marc & Sue are very big on irony.

The couple think of themselves as post-political. They care about the universe. In the course of their work they spend a fair amount of time nipping between continents, and consequently identify more with their professional counterparts in New York and Tokyo than with some small geographical concept like a country. They like the area they live in; although, as Sue says, it is rather *white*.

Both of them have done a good job of kicking away their moorings, all the better to realise their own, unique qualities. They rarely see their families – they have little in common with them now. And besides, the two of them are strictly organic, and Sue has her allergies, which means that invitations to Sunday lunch have to be got round as graciously as possible. And now that Sue is pregnant, they're anyway having to ponder the ways in which they'll have to restructure and reposition their Lifestyles. At the moment, they're preoccupied with what to call the kid. Sid, or Harold maybe, if it's a boy – gently post-modern and, of course, nicely ironic.

* * * * *

Jason is beside himself with rage. That rude bloke on the train asked him to take his feet off the seat opposite. Why didn't he just sit somewhere else? What's his problem?

Jason spends a lot of time on trains and buses, listening to his iPod. Today he's been to get his eyebrow piercing cleaned up. He can't work, because he's been diagnosed with severe unhappiness. In any case, he can't find a job that fits his needs. He can't handle being told what to do. It does his head in.

* * * * *

These characters and incidents are fictitious. However, as they say in the movies, they are based on real people and real events, in that they would be recognisable to most of us – as friends, acquaintances, or simply as types we come up against every day. Kayleigh's shenanigans might exasperate many of us; Jason might fill us with anger or even fear. Some of us might aspire to the kind of life Harriet lives; others might consider that Marc & Sue have got it all just right. But none of them would strike us as especially remarkable in their behaviour, beliefs or attitudes to themselves. They are all of them utterly familiar.

Not that this would please them. Because, whether unconsciously or not, Harriet, Jason, Marc & Sue and Kayleigh in their own ways all think of themselves as extraordinary. They are without category. They would be horrified to be described as a 'type'. They are, after all, unique. Society, if it exists at all – and they would probably not give it a second thought – is something that should be bent and moulded to their requirements. It should recognise their desires, listen to their views, and appreciate their particular gifts.

They may operate at different levels and may be unaware of each other's worlds, but they are bound together by a similar belief: they all consider themselves *special*.

Of course, few would disagree that the need most of us feel to be appreciated by others – by our family, our friends and peers – is natural and healthy. The desire to be well-thought of can act both as a spur to individual achievement, and as the glue that keeps society together. Striving to be top in the field, to hone a particular talent – or simply to make money, if that's your chosen path – can be inspiring and attractive.

But the need to be *special*, to be taken uncritically at one's own self-evaluation, or to draw attention to oneself at every opportunity, is something else entirely. Claiming uniqueness – regardless of talent or deed – by making oneself the most seen, by shouting the loudest, or simply by means of brute force, might give the individual satisfaction (although this alone is highly questionable); but the effect on society's morale can be both destructive and divisive.

It can be heard right there in the language. It's fair to say that the traditional British trait of self-effacement has gone the way of the bowler hat. Be understated now about your work ('Oh, it keeps the wolf from the door'), or what you have done with your life ('this and that'), and you will be taken at your word. For many modern Britons, raised to cherish self-esteem above all else, such modesty is simply not understood or is tantamount to self-negation, the greatest crime of all. Hyperbole rules the day, regardless of the banality of the circumstances: I'm devastated, you're *totally* incredible, he's *completely* bizarre.

Putting yourself at the centre of the universe, childlike as it is, is not in modern Britain a habit restricted to would-be stars, surly youths and hyped-up urban professionals. Educated middle-class types do it in more rarefied ways, although the effect is the same in the end. Despite the ever-increasing use in the media of the word 'community' – and indeed, despite what would appear to be a nostalgia for the simplicities of the past – there is, in fact, a repudiation among some sections of the population of any form of collective identity, whether expressed in nationhood, locality or personal roots. Such concepts are seen as constricting by these single, soaring selves. Fascinated by other cultures, from which they carefully cherry-pick, and fans on principle of anything that transgresses the 'norm', they are self-designated Citizens of the World, flattering themselves with their love of 'the other'. Totally self-formed (at least in their own eyes), they can shine forth, unsullied by any form of limiting group membership. Even when they do something as collective as a political protest – 'Not in My Name!' – it is still resolutely egotistical.

Not that a group in itself is a bar to being special – so long as it's the right one of course. If you can claim victimhood of one variety or another – and according to a recent report, that's upwards of 70 per cent of us – you, too, can count yourself special. If that fails, then you can always exploit your emotional life for the benefit of the cameras – or perhaps latch onto somebody else's grief.

But it is in the cult of celebrity – which could, arguably, be better renamed the cult of visibility – that we can see the most glaring manifestation of what we might call the flight from ordinariness in modern British culture. To witness the elevation of the nonentity from mostly well-deserved obscurity to a position in which he or she receives blanket coverage from tabloid and broadsheet alike – as happens most obviously in so-called reality television – is an utterly demoralising and draining experience. Our attention is forced onto people and events that would otherwise barely register in our thoughts, and in the process our own everyday priorities, concerns and efforts are demeaned and diminished. Jade Goody's effect on us has not, ultimately, been an elevating one.

The current obsession with celebrity is at odds with the broader landscape of British culture, which has traditionally prided itself on being less susceptible to such things. It exists now purely as an end in itself: the flip side of our own obsession with ourselves. Celebrity is seen by thousands as an utterly attainable state, a tradable commodity. The more level-headed might be amused by the passing circus. Even those with a modicum of self-awareness would be able to put a distance between it and themselves. Marc & Sue would doubtless read the odd *Hello!* magazine, albeit ironically. But for the less well-equipped, like Kayleigh, brought up to believe that all must have prizes, there really is no hope. And if, like Jason, they feel they've been told they are infinitely capable and then cheated of their place in the game, they might even get violent.

Should any of this matter? If you worry about the gradual disintegration of the public arena, then yes, it matters. If you are one of those people who find themselves slowly but surely abandoning visits to restaurants, cinemas and theatres, exhausted by the loud exhibitionism and selfishness that pass for 'vibrancy', then yes, it matters. If you despair at the debasement of both our culture and its belief in the importance and capacity of the individual, then yes, it matters. If you believe that an attachment to something bigger than just our own selves is vital not only for social cohesion but also for inner balance, then it matters hugely.

A couple of years ago, the Prince of Wales, in his typically plaintive way, bemoaned the fashion for out-of-control self-belief. 'What is wrong with everybody nowadays?' he complained in a leaked memo. 'What is it that makes everyone seem to think they are qualified to do things far beyond their technical capabilities?' Predictably and wilfully misrepresented, the Prince was torn limb from limb by the media, which saw only aristocratic *de haut en bas*. But you didn't need to be remotely privileged to see that he'd put his finger on something. His remarks sparked a few days' discussion about the failings of the education system. Vitally important though that is, it's not the whole story. If the Prince feels like venturing into further enquiry, then I'd recommend to him the following thoughts and observations.

CHAPTER THREE

KAYLEIGH'S WORLD

I'm gonna live forever,
I'm gonna learn how to fly,
I feel it coming together,
People will see me and cry
I'm gonna make it to heaven,
Light up the sky like a flame
I'm gonna live forever,
Baby remember my name.
Remember, remember, remember, etc., etc.

Lyrics from *Fame* (1980)

One person who has recently joined the celebrity line-up at Tussauds is Simon Cowell. This is probably appropriate, as Cowell is better known on both sides of the Atlantic than any of the 'singing sensations' he has created through talent shows like the *X Factor* and *American Idol* – programmes in which he in reality is the star and which make him millions every year. He's been mocked for his high-waisted trousers, his vanity and his so-called man-boobs. He bulks very large in Kayleigh's world.

It's Cowell's alleged meanness to the hundreds who come to audition that has made him notorious. He doesn't see it this way, of course. 'I haven't done anything particularly harsh', he has said. 'Harshness to me is giving somebody false hopes and not following through. Telling some guy or some girl who's got zero talent that they have zero talent actually is a kindness.'

Of course, the way Cowell lets them know has much to do with the hostility he arouses. At times, he wields a giant hammer even when the nut is obviously already cracked. But he should be forgiven this; for, in an age when the duty to be special, to stand out, to be above all else *visible*, is more vigorously adhered to than any other, he is providing what amounts to a valuable and desperately needed public service.

Cowell built his own fortune, and so is not open to the same attacks that rained down on Prince Charles, when his why-oh-why memo was leaked to the press. Cowell made his money in the pop music business, and so presumably knows what he is talking about.

Over the past few years, he has weathered the self-pitying tears of hundreds of tuneless would-be entertainers, many of whom appeared to have committed to memory the contents of a shelf of self-help books. Sometimes he has even been forced to square up to parents who are outraged at his dismissal of their offspring's unique creative gifts, and whose wrath can be something to behold. Many of the contestants themselves advance in the apparent belief that a simple (yet endless) repetition of their need to fulfil their dreams, a constant reiteration of their desperately held desires ('Please! Please! I *know* I can do this!'), should in itself be enough to take them on to the next stage in the process. And if Cowell and his fellow judges fail to concur, the wannabes can sometimes turn nasty. 'They're so aggressive!' whispered his fellow panellist, Sharon Osbourne, to camera during a lull in the auditions in one programme.

Cowell's is just the best known voice to emerge from television's current love affair with all forms of contest. Pitting willing amateurs against each other fits perfectly both with its current obsession with the trappings – if not the substance – of fame, and with its celebration (witness the explosion of reality TV) of the nonentity culture – paradoxically at a time when the public voice, as heard through news and current affairs programmes, has largely disappeared. Whether it's to be told 'You're fired!' by Alan Sugar in *The Apprentice*, or to be proclaimed the heir to Julie Andrews in *How Do You Solve a Problem Like Maria?*, and despite the limited shelf life of the kind of celebrity created by such programmes, thousands continue to present themselves, to wave in unison at the cameras, as they queue 10 abreast, waiting to be seen and – hopefully – discovered. Such has been the popularity of these shows that they have been credited with reviving a whole tradition of variety-led entertainment on television; at the same time, they have been condemned as exercises in crass populist sadism – the equivalent of throwing Christians to lions. And it can certainly look that way when you witness superannuated teenagers being reduced to an apparent contemplation of suicide on being judged to be 'not right for this part'.

But perhaps such critics are missing the point. In a culture driven half crazy by easy empathy and even easier credit, Cowell and his colleagues are providing an outlet (no doubt totally unconsciously) for our distant tribal memory that, however tough the struggle, to be the best or the most talented is a Good Thing; and that spending your time softening the pain of others might make you feel warm inside in the short term, but will eventually lead to a landscape barren of genuine, inspiring achievement. Cowell talks to the huddled masses who come before him – all of them convinced they have that special extra something – as equals. The last thing he can be accused of being is patronising. But in today's topsy-turvy climate, it is the straight-between-the-eyes advice he hands out, his lack of fluffy touchy-feeliness, that exposes him to charges of condescension from those for whom being 'judgemental' is the greatest sin of all. In the case of possibly hundreds of these would-be stars, his judgement is probably the first really helpful criticism they've ever heard. Suppressed for so long in the name of engineering a more 'fulfilled' society, a smothered competitive instinct has seeped out onto the TV screen of all places, and hence right back into the centre of our lives.

PLEASE LEAVE THE HOUSE

The same cannot be said of reality shows like *Big Brother* and its countless imitators. It is easy to dismiss these sorry programmes as exercises in smirking voyeurism, a return to the cruel lunatic-baiting of past centuries. It's also a comforting way of explaining away a phenomenon that most of us would otherwise find hard to comprehend: the willing submission of oneself to the ridicule and enforced company of a bunch of strangers in the 24-hour glare of television cameras. Of course, the lunatics had no choice in the matter; whereas, in the case of *Big Brother*, thousands upon thousands apply in the hope that simply by being seen to exist, however tawdrily, they will become household names. And it works, for a while. It's unlikely that Jade Goody will ever have heard of Andy Warhol or his prediction that, in the future, everyone would be famous for 15 minutes; yet she is living proof that he was onto something – not, of course, that Andy was bargaining on somebody like Jade.

The visibility achieved by the *Big Brother* contestants might be fleeting, but it is intense. Like an assassin or serial killer, the face of the winner – or a popular loser – will, for some weeks or months, be the most recognisable in the country. It will adorn the pages of the countless new magazines that have sprung up like penny dreadfuls over the past few years and are devoted to the comings and goings of celebrity plankton; and it will appear in the tabloids and the broadsheets that hide behind them. The emotional histories, the all-round niceness, the very *ordinariness* of people like Chantelle will be analysed and dissected. Colour spreads will fill the weekend supplements. The contestants will be invited to turn up at premiers and launches, and their pictures will take precedence over those of established movie stars in the next morning's papers.

The fact that they have done nothing for their fame, other than to be themselves in front of a camera, is treated as though it is in itself some kind of endearing quality, worthy of celebration. Having maybe been dismissed as participants in a freak show, they are then treated as figures deemed worthy of our attention. Their pronouncements make headlines; and when things go badly awry, as when Goody exposed herself as an ignorant bully and sparked an international diplomatic row in the process, their views and actions are reported with the same weight as if they were emanating from politicians.

To sensible eyes, reality-show contestants who hit the jackpot may appear to be a bunch of social and intellectual inadequates. But when they achieve their 15 minutes of shame, they themselves show no obvious embarrassment or self-consciousness over their lack of attainment. In this, they are arguably nearer to the popular spirit of the time than we might care to admit. This *Zeitgeist* is one that confuses crude exhibitionism with colourful flamboyance, coarse rudeness with 'authenticity', self-belief with self-knowledge, aggression with strength. It makes little distinction between notoriety and fame – probably correctly, because, in a society with a disintegrating moral framework, the very concept of notoriety becomes redundant. Most of all, it is a spirit which sees public visibility as an end in itself, regardless of talent or distinction, and which encourages attention-seeking as an aid to individual self-expression. And for Kayleigh, getting her practice in with her friends in their hired limo, the logical conclusion of this is the fame game. And she wants a piece of it.

MORE STARS THAN THERE ARE IN HEAVEN

She is trying to join an increasingly crowded landscape. It's a cliché that we live in a time in which celebrity-worship has reached fever pitch; that never before have we been so in thrall to the famous. It seems odd, then, that, despite the thousands of 'personalities' clogging up the airwaves, there is nobody around who could attract the kind of crowds who greeted the Beatles when they arrived at JFK airport on their first American tour, or spark the riot of mourning that followed the death of Rudolph Valentino. If there is a public obsession, then it would seem to be a particularly passive one. What is more likely is that the very nature of fame has changed, and with the ubiquity of celebrity has come a shift in our attitude and our relationship to it.

Not so long ago, when living in Los Angeles and browsing through a Hollywood memorabilia shop, I came across a batch of transfixing old photos. They were copies of one of the best known fashion advertising campaigns of the post-war years, for Blackglama furs. The famous tagline – 'What Becomes a Legend Most?' – was all that accompanied this series of black and white portraits, dating mostly from the 1960s and 1970s, of such stars as Marlene Dietrich, Sophia Loren and Rudolf Nureyev. In their sophistication and beauty, these people seemed like creatures from another planet; but what was really striking was the sense of sheer adultness that they exuded. It was this, with its suggestion of worldliness, achievement and humour, that gave them their glamour.

As a definition of stardom, this has virtually disappeared. 'Glamour' to the modern eye is not some unique, magical quality that we might glimpse in the famous studio portraits of Garbo by Clarence Sinclair Bull, in the almost regal gracefulness that studios such as MGM inculcated in their huge stable of 1940s stars, or in the unattainable talent and physical charisma of a Margot Fonteyn or a Maria Callas. It has become, instead, almost purely a matter of make-up and frocks. As such, it is an image, like 'sporty' or the ridiculous 'smart casual', which can be acquired by everybody. It is a consumer option, albeit one that comes without the public recognisability factor. Other-worldliness has nothing to do with it. The image might be based on the particular look of a certain celebrity, and the public might still want to imitate it. But they are no longer in awe of stars. The celebrity is increasingly seen simply as one of us who got lucky, who got visible; and above all else, the 'fans' want familiarity with him or her – to appear to be part of his or her world. And it starts early: Jake Halpern, the American author of *Fame Junkies*, found that, when given a list of 10 options for future careers, a massive 43 per cent of schoolchildren in the USA wanted to be a 'celebrity personal assistant'. So much for space travel.

The increasingly intrusive, 24-hour media are usually blamed for demystifying stardom; but this is really only a small part of the explanation. Much of the reason for the transformation in our attitude to fame must be laid at the door of the youth obsession, which, from its beginnings in the 1950s, has grown to the point where it now constitutes the mainstream culture. Being grown up is a prerequisite for possessing true glamour. The celebrities who twinkle in our current firmament might be sexy, buff, quirky or full of elfin energy, but adult they are not. We live a million light years away from the knowing rakishness of Gable and Lombard, the old-world bearing of Olivier and Leigh, or even the diamond-encrusted panache of Burton and Taylor. With few exceptions, our stars have a provincial, B-movie quality, like superannuated prom kings and queens.

An enormous amount of time and effort goes into making sure contemporary stars do indeed appear 'down' with the fans, large contingents of whom have swallowed this whole. (Of course, as anybody who has worked the showbiz PR circuit knows, the truth is that these celebrities, especially those of the established counter-culture variety, are generally more vain, more status-conscious and more self-regarding than any of the raft of regal 'golden age' stars that preceded them.) In our current culture, youth is held to be democratic, well-intentioned, caring and – above all – *interesting*; and as such the stars and their keepers assiduously highlight these qualities when cultivating their public images.

The appearance of youth is everything. It is astonishing to realise that when, as Rhett Butler, Gable was proclaiming wearily to Scarlett that, quite frankly, he couldn't give a damn, he was six years younger than our own perpetual juvenile lead, Tom Cruise. Gable was recognisably a man of the world; Cruise remains an unchanging, narcissistic Peter Pan figure with the weightlessness of a college grad. Similarly, the difference between the suave reliability of the pristine Cary Grant and the sputtering tentativeness of his supposed modern incarnation, Hugh Grant, shows how, no matter how grown up one might appear, it is nowadays required that, in matters of screen behaviour, it is best to defer to the child within.

The out-of-control cult of youth, with its desperate need to praise the shiny, the new and, above all else, the sexy, has in the past four decades stealthily robbed us of a sense that adultness is something to be aspired to.

'Our obsession with youth is not new, but it's definitely accelerated', Morris Berman, author of *The Twilight of American Culture*, once told me during an interview about this phenomenon. Looking at US culture in Freudian terms, he said, one could see how the adult part of the psyche, the superego, had, since the 1960s, effectively been discarded, leaving only the id – that part which represented selfish, child-like desires. 'Infants want to be entertained and tend to resist education', he went on. 'Compare movies from the 50s with those of the 90s. Just in terms of camera time for conversation, those from the 50s moved slowly, and people talked. Now, the length of sentences is short, and that's because a child's attention span is so short.'

Film is still the dominant medium, of course, and it remains the most sure-fire way of passing the Bogart test ('You're not a star until they can spell your name in Karachi'). But the change in the overall nature of celebrity has meant that our era has seen a greater separation than ever between talent and fame. Figures of huge distinction might come and go in the worlds of ballet, opera and theatre, but it is increasingly unlikely that they will ever achieve the household-name status enjoyed in bygone times by Fonteyn, Nureyev, Callas or even Jacqueline du Pré – stars who were known even to those who had never set foot in an opera house or concert hall. Similarly, it is hard to imagine now an actress achieving fame as a first lady of the West End Stage. The days when the theatre made its own stars – stars who were as familiar to the general public as any movie idol – are well and truly over.

THE GREATEST LOVE OF ALL

Berman might have added that it is another attribute of childhood to see yourself as being the centre of the universe. Despite its supposedly altruistic politics, much of the so-called counter-culture of the Sixties – which has since become the reigning orthodoxy – relied for its appeal on middle-class, self-important, adolescent contrariness. Similarly, pop culture (as opposed to popular culture in its broadest sense) has relentlessly exploited and celebrated youthful emotional self-dramatisation and the desire for what is now called 'peer-group recognition'. 'I am beautiful, no matter what they say/ Words can't bring me down', sang Christina Aguilera, a decade or so after Whitney Houston urged us passionately (if ungrammatically) that 'Learning to love yourself/It is the greatest love of all'. Just pop songs, perhaps; but not so easy to dismiss when one considers that they could well be used as anthems by the ever-burgeoning self-help industry and by a therapy culture which sees critical judgement, when applied to the individual, as the greatest sin of all.

Kayleigh will have taken all this to heart, even if subconsciously. She is still young enough to have formed the belief, inspired perhaps by *Big Brother*, that all she needs to do to be special is to make sure other people realise it. It's also more than likely that she will have been part of an educational system that flattered her uniqueness and put her firmly at the centre of what is now known as the 'learning', rather than the 'teaching', process. In *All Must Have Prizes*, her excellent study of how the educational establishment has betrayed Britain's children, Melanie Phillips describes how the 'child-centred' orthodoxy that has been dogmatically adhered to during much of the post-war period purported to benefit children through an enhanced respect for their individuality, but actually had the opposite effect:

> It tells us that we have thrown overboard the authority of external rules. We have decided that relevance, context and localised experience are what really matter. Instead of authority being located 'out there' in a body of knowledge handed down through centuries, we have repositioned it 'in here' within each child. In doing so, we have deprived those children of the structures through which human beings have traditionally made sense of the world. Instead, children are having to make it up for themselves as they go along. They are being abandoned to disorder, incoherence and flux.

Those of us whose experience is of the state education system can all come up with examples of this disorder, incoherence and flux. A close relative of mine, a teaching assistant, was encouraged to make sure that her pupils clapped heartily when one of their number simply answered a question correctly. On another occasion, a girl who came first in a simple class exam was given a Top Shop voucher as a prize. It is surely no wonder that the notion of teachers as figures of respect is virtually obsolete; your average child can sense when it is being cajoled, flattered and bribed – when it is being given a pre-eminence which, it senses, it hasn't really earned.

The idea that bringing out the innate creativity of each child should take absolute precedence over properly equipping it with the powers of reason and analysis – in Phillips's words, 'teaching it to think' – results in a chaos that makes a mockery of real creative endeavour. She makes this important point:

> Creativity is like freedom itself: it flourishes only
> within a clear framework of moral and intellectual
> boundaries. Remove the enclosing structures and all
> that remains is a vacuum of anarchic impulses which
> are deeply hostile to creativity. Many of the greatest
> figures of English and world culture, after all, were
> subjected to precisely the kind of rigid educational
> disciplines that so offend contemporary educationalists.
> Conversely, we have hardly lived through a new
> renaissance of creative endeavour since the elevation of
> creativity to its pedestal in British education; on the
> contrary, our culture is atrophying beneath the weight
> of the second- and third-rate.

It is hardly surprising that one of the results of this disastrous educational policy has been a cultural atmosphere in which aspiration towards external knowledge – or even the development of a genuine self-knowledge acquired in a collective context – is disdained, mocked and considered to be both irrelevant and a barrier to the unfettered expression of the desires and feelings of the individual. And competition in this context is consequently seen as the cruellest blow of all. The possibility that a child might be exposed to the fact that there are others who can run faster, or have a greater aptitude for languages, or have a superior natural talent for drawing, is seen as damaging and something from which that child should be shielded.

Not that all parents are fighting this. In fact, many of them have inwardly and maybe unconsciously imbibed the so-called 'anti-repression' school of child-rearing, which first came into vogue in the Fifties, to the point that any form of restriction is nowadays seen as somehow harmful to their offspring's potential. As a result, many children are growing up not just ill-disciplined but actually unsocialised on a more fundamental level. A couple of viewings of TV series such as the BBC's *Honey, We're Killing the Kids* can leave one profoundly depressed: not because of the food intake of the families taking part (which is ostensibly the point of the show), but because of the way in which the whims, likes and dislikes of the children have become the rules by which life is led. It is not necessary to be the child-catcher to be utterly exasperated at the way in which so many are now allowed to dominate most social situations, public places and even conversations. And woe betide the fearless individual who raises an objection. The child is seen as some delicate little flower, just waiting to be damaged by outside forces; and it is no overstatement to say that many parents appear positively terrified in case some action on their part will stunt the emotional capacity – and perhaps limitless talent – of their little Kayleigh.

So, if you have been effectively deprived of the proper tools and mental discipline required first to develop any real understanding of the world around you, and then to go on and perhaps make your mark, what is open to you?

IF YOU'VE GOT IT, FLAUNT IT…AND IF YOU HAVEN'T, FLAUNT IT ANYWAY

Celebrity might be a long-term aim of Kayleigh's, but while she's waiting there is time to fill. Go to any city centre or market town on a Friday or Saturday night and you'll see how she might be doing it. Mass socialising – centred around binge-drinking – has become a stage on which to live out your fantasies and draw as much attention to yourself as possible. And that – despite all the outward signs on show of a rollicking good time, despite the crowds, the noise and the shrieks of laughter emanating from under the flocks of ever-present glittery Stetsons – might explain the oddly mirthless atmosphere that is so often attendant.

'Parading' is the name that the writer Francis Gilbert gave to this now ever-present feature of British public life. During his travels around the country researching his book, *Yob Nation*, he asked one female reveller in night-time Swansea what she got out of the whole thing:

It's the dressing up. It's the becoming someone else. It's walking up and down and showing everyone what you're made of. It's being proud of who you are. It's not caring at all. It's not giving a fuck any more.

Gilbert saw different forms of this parading, in all social environments where young people gathered, and across all social milieus. Our need to join the yobs' parade, he said, is what makes us British. If this claim is as true as it is depressing, there has been a fundamental change in national character. That there has always been a pronounced aggressive streak in much of public life in this country is without question. Comparisons between our own time and Hogarth's 18th century are regularly trotted out by commentators determined to prove that nothing has really changed; the English have always had a yobbish quality, which comes to the fore after a stint of industrial drinking on the town. The difference now is that this is accompanied by a deathly determination on the part of the individual to prove to others – to anybody –

that, by hook or by crook, he (or she) will be taken notice of.

Going further afield to the notorious Cypriot holiday resort of Ayia Napa, a place especially favoured by young Brits, Gilbert witnessed a couple having sex in a swimming pool, in full view of everybody. On expressing his incredulity to a fellow drinker, he got the following answer:

> That girl has probably been planning for a moment like this for months... She's spent all day, from the moment she's got up, deciding on her costume and where she'll go with her mates. And then when she's gone out she's felt everyone's eyes on her and she's loved it. It's like there's a holiday spirit that has turned you into a model or something...she's not anything special, she's not that pretty, and yet she's pulled that muscly guy. She'd never get a guy like him back home, but here all the normal rules are suspended. It's about being in your own little Big Brother reality TV show. Being watched makes you feel special, like a media star, a celebrity.

This girl was a big fish in a small pond (literally), but she was just one example of the current urgent need to display, to exhibit, to make sure others know you are there, which runs counter to the traditionally held view of the British as valuing understatement in both behaviour and speech – even maybe when drunk.

The notion that self-effacement, modesty and a horror of social embarrassment are all qualities which characterise the British is one that lingers, even when simple everyday experience points to the fact that these things are no longer valued or adhered to by many of us. Play down your career successes or your emotional turmoil, keep yourself (and your feelings) to yourself, don't make a fuss, and you will, increasingly, be taken at face value. We have embraced the belief that, in order to exist, one has to be seen (and heard) to exist.

It is arguable that this is one of the results of a society that has kicked away its past structures and that is, at least on the face of it, more meritocratic. The fact that there is much evidence to show that this simply is not the case, and that social mobility has actually declined quite dramatically over the past couple of decades – especially among people like Kayleigh and her friends – is immaterial, for the perception that 'it's all up to you' is widespread. As the psychologist Oliver James has pointed out:

> Your job or career is critical for identity in this situation. The question 'what do you do?' is almost indistinguishable from the one 'who are you?' Mothers who dare to leave paid employment and care for small children full time discover this: suddenly, they have the status of something less than a road-sweeper.

Traditional explanations for under-achievement or social invisibility, which were often based on the drawbacks of one's class background, are seen increasingly as excuses for personal failings. Being modest or self-effacing is not going to cut it in this environment, and neither is showing consideration towards those who toil in menial jobs or who appear socially invisible. If you're over 40, it's easy to recall a time when it was a matter of simple good manners to be polite to ticket collectors, shop assistants, drivers and those who earned their living doing hard or repetitive manual tasks. Now such positions are scorned, considered beneath contempt, and dismissed as McJobs. The common use of the contemporary insult 'Loser!' to describe such people is proof of how desperately many of us need to distance ourselves from the perceived failures of others.

ARE YOU 'AVING A LAUGH?

This attitude is reflected in aspects of the popular culture we enjoy. It can be detected most easily in the things we choose to laugh at. The current fashion for the so-called comedy of cruelty paradoxically grew out of the politically correct, supposedly victim-sensitive, invariably anti-conservative alternative comedy of the 1980s. The feeling which runs through much of it is contempt for the ordinary and the un-hip; it prefers to laugh at people, as opposed to their foibles.

Comparisons have been made between Rickie Gervais, who played David Brent in the popular comedy series *The Office*, and Tony Hancock. Both drew for much of their material on the mundane and the commonplace – the rituals and humiliations of everyday life, the death by a thousand cuts. The crucial difference was that, in portraying the frustrations of Everyman, Hancock made his audience laugh *with* him. It was on his side because it recognised humanity and affection when it saw it. *The Office*, by contrast, though cleverly written and superbly acted, appealed to the contemporary desire to laugh at the delusions and pettiness all of us are prone to in order to get through life – not from a sense of shared familiarity, but from a position of smirking superiority. How pathetic these people are! What losers!

Similarly, the comic creations of the late Dick Emery – the suburban vamp, the camp queen, the frustrated spinster – linger even now in the popular imagination, because they endeared themselves to us. This was largely because they were performed by Emery with a real warmth. The characters of *Little Britain*, on the other hand, are mostly hateful – grotesques we are invited to laugh at, even as we are simultaneously disgusted by them. Surprisingly old-hat targets, such as the Women's Institute, are resurrected and re-heated, so that scorn can be poured on them anew for their supposed prejudices; and fresh ones – Vicky Pollard, the underclass teenage mother – are added in a spirit of unalloyed snobbery (it's one of the media mysteries of our time how this show managed to brand itself as politically incorrect; mostly steering clear of poking fun at black and Asian characters, and with its knowing, ironic treatment of gays, it couldn't have been more PC).

This comedy is essentially anti-communal; it seems to be saying: 'Thank God that you, laughing at this, are not like these people.' Much of the laughter it generates is of the hollow kind one hears when an audience is determined to laugh simply to make a point, to show that it is 'on side'. It is hardly surprising, either, that the series should show signs of starting to fade rapidly from the public's memory. Its appeal is based on the exploitation of the audience's vanity. And that provides too superficial a basis for the show genuinely to last in the public's affections in a way that, for example, *Dad's Army* has – a programme so much of which was a celebration of understatement, the gentle debunking of pomposity, and the everyday efforts of ordinary people.

YOUR PAIN IS MY PAIN, YOUR TEARS ARE MY TEARS

'If you didn't laugh, you'd cry' – a saying Kayleigh might well have heard from her parents. And now there are countless opportunities for her to do that, too, and put herself right there in the middle of the action. If it's attention she wants, there's no need for her to go spilling her guts out about her torrid, squalid emotional life on a TV talk show, for there is a whole self-aggrandising sentimentality industry out there now at her disposal.

It would have been nice to have got through a whole book such as this without mentioning the 'D word', but one must admit defeat. Reams have been written about the public reaction to the death of Princess Diana a decade ago, and how it proved that the nation had fundamentally changed in its attitudes, responses and public behaviour. If you didn't weep, you were obviously repressed, cold and inhuman; an undemonstrative disposition was proof of what we might call 'emotion crime', and there was no way of answering the charge (just ask the Queen). But not all agree: in her exhaustively researched book, *Watching the English*, the social anthropologist Kate Fox concluded that the occasion had, in fact, shown how the British had remained much the same: they queued for hours to sign books of condolence; and, by and large, they watched in dignified silence as the coffin went past, only throwing flowers onto the hearse once the main ceremonial was over. It's a nice idea, but it fails to convince.

For much of the hysterical reaction to Diana's death – as heard in comments made by weeping mourners to the TV cameras and newspapers, not to mention the countless circular candle-holding sessions – showed that possibly hundreds of thousands of people took the opportunity to display and dramatise not necessarily a love for the Princess, but their own current sense of self-worth, their own emotional traumas, and their own problems. The death of this public figure simply gave them a stage and a spotlight. And, as Libby Purves wrote in *The Times* on the 10th anniversary of the event, it also unleashed a vile, bullying reaction to those who were, ironically, the most connected to the death:

> It was horrible. Horrible because, whatever their complex feelings about Diana, the experience of the Balmoral [Royal] party was real. This was the mother of two loved grandchildren, the wife for a decade of a troubled son. Real grief, real shock, is nothing like the vicarious sort. It is disorientating, hollow, private; it contains strange pockets of numbness, even of hope. The bereaved need to be private or among close friends, if only because their behaviour may be counterintuitive: they may even laugh at ironies or incongruities (ask any undertaker). They do not need to be put on display, looking stricken for the benefit of onlookers. Not until the funeral, at least. Anyone should know that.

In the 10 years since then, the country has become used to regular bouts of emotional incontinence – over Louise Woodward, the Soham murders – and good luck to anybody who tries to stem the flow. Only recently, with the debacle over the Iran naval hostages, has there been the slightest inkling that a few qualms may be surfacing over what we have become. Seaman Fay Turney's claim that *her* story had to be told – which she then did, with an apparent lack of self-consciousness as to its total self-centredness – helped provoke a backlash, although normal service was resumed shortly afterwards with the disappearance of Madeleine McCann. These headline cases might, of course, be led by the media; but it would be unfair to say that they are solely creations of the media: in many respects, the papers are simply reflecting what has changed 'on the street'.

Grief has become another way of putting on a show. As I write these words, there are no fewer than three flowery shrines within walking distance in my part of South East London, bedecked with fluffy toys and photographs. It is hard not to be made uncomfortable by the extravagant claims made for the deceased – in each case, young people who were involved in traffic accidents – and by the odd way in which the whole display intrudes on one's own private thoughts. Doubtless there is sincerity there; but one battles against the uncharitable thought that these shrines, with their childlike sense of drama, provide the perfect opportunity for those for whom private grief is no grief at all to show off to the outside world.

The determination of others, possibly complete strangers, to add their all-important tuppence worth can also lead to embarrassing situations: one letter to the satirical magazine *Private Eye* described how the writer had placed a wrongly delivered bouquet of flowers next to a nearby lamppost in the hope that it would be claimed, only to find, when he returned home later, that it had been joined by four more bunches. Another related an incident in Liverpool, where someone had found what appeared to be an aborted foetus in a back street. Soon the site was covered in flowers, teddy bears and maudlin messages – until the Merseyside Police announced that the remains were, in fact, those of a chicken.

With her youthful, heightened sense of self-dramatisation, Kayleigh probably already knows what she'd like played at her own funeral. Fair enough for an 18-year-old, you might say – except that more and more of us are not, apparently, leaving to chance the weird and wonderful ways in which we want to be remembered. At the turn of the millennium, BBC News Online covered a report commissioned by the Co-operative Funeral Service, which revealed a growing demand for personal, custom-made ceremonies, in which religion, and with it the implied sense of the deceased in some sort of external context, would play less and less of a part.

'Whether it is a particular version of a pop song or a horse-drawn hearse, we want to have the last word in how we are remembered and personalise our funeral by exercising the wide number of options available to us', said a Co-operative spokesman, as a new service devoted to carrying out all the deceased's detailed demands, the Funeral Pledge, was launched. Chart-topping 'power ballads' are increasingly taking over from traditional hymns, with Bette Midler's 'Wind Beneath My Wings', and Celine Dion's 'My Heart Will Go On' featuring among the most consistently popular choices.

When the time comes for Kayleigh's wingéd heart to take off from this earthly runway, many of us might wince simply at the aesthetics of it all. 'Strange how potent cheap music is', mused Noël Coward; but even he would certainly have balked at the use of 'Mad About the Boy' at his memorial service – and he wrote it. Others will ponder their discomfiture, caused perhaps by that distant remembered instinct, lodged at the back of their minds, which tells them that there should be more to it than this.

CHAPTER FOUR

HARRIET'S WORLD

...for the growing good of the world is partly dependent
on unhistoric acts; and that things are not so ill with
you and me as they might have been, is half owing to
the number who lived faithfully a hidden life, and rest in
unvisited tombs.

George Eliot, Middlemarch

'I was like, Okaaay, so you're a member of your local history
society. I'm like, how sad is that! He was kind of cute,
actually, but I'm so totally not going to spend my weekends
trudging round old bloody ruins. Actually, I think he was,
like, quite religious, too, and I was like, *Hello!*'

Over a glass of chilled Chardonnay after work, Harriet is
explaining to her girlfriends why last Friday's date was ultimately a bit of a waste of time. In fact, it's more accurate to
say she is explaining to one particular friend on her mobile,
while the other three sit grinning, waiting for her to finish. In
any case, they all, like, totally get it.

The idea that an individual might have an interest,
much less a passion or strong belief, which exists outside of
himself, which relates to conditions, ideas or circumstances
not immediately connected to a fascination with his own
character and desires, is something that, for many people,
especially younger urban types, is increasingly difficult to
comprehend. There are exceptions to this – football, of
course, and global pop causes that come and go, like Live 8,
which are anyway all about showing off your moral superiority. But as a general rule, the thought that one might be part

of something that will in any way dilute one's individuality, one's *special-ness*, by necessarily putting oneself at the service of something wider, is now alien to millions.

SAD FACTS

This is reflected in the gradual erosion of most forms of collective public activity in recent decades. Membership of political parties has been in freefall, with both major parties now having fewer than 500,000 members between them – a tenth, astonishingly, of the level in the 1950s. A YouGov poll of some 2,500 adults across Britain in 2007, commissioned by the Royal Society for the Encouragement of Arts, Manufactures and Commerce (RSA), revealed that this simply mirrored a more general, steep decline in other forms of civic activity. Seven out of 10 people have no ties to groups or associations in their neighbourhood, and in the 18–24-year-old group, this figure rises to eight out of 10. A mere 8 per cent are involved with a religious organisation (less than 7 per cent attend church regularly), and only 6 per cent with a local charity. Just 5 per cent are involved with a residents' association, 4 per cent with a youth or student group, and 3 per cent with the Scouts or Guides; in fact, membership of the Scout Association has fallen by a third since the early 1990s. Slipping further and further down the scale of collective activity are book groups at just 2 per cent, and, at 1 per cent, Rotary Clubs, trading associations and baby-sitting circles. And membership of the Women's Institute, now standing at 215,000, has spectacularly halved since the 1970s.

The main reasons offered by those questioned for their lack of involvement were lack of time (45 per cent) and a lack of 'relevant' groups (28 per cent). The chief executive of the RSA, Matthew Taylor, claimed that the survey showed the failure of traditional organisations to adapt to modern lifestyles. 'There were community organisations that were very powerful in the post-war period, but don't seem to fit the way people operate today', he told the *Daily Telegraph*.

I think people are saying that they haven't got much time, and they are only willing if they can do something that they can see the immediate value of. The issue is how we develop new forms of community organisations which enable people to act on issues they care about, without having to be involved in committee meetings and bureaucracy.

Mr Taylor was being kind. The truth is, of course, that in real terms they *do* have time. It is not about work: figures from the Office for National Statistics show that, in the past decade alone, the average working week has shortened from 39 to 37.5 hours. Rather, more people now make the calculation that after the demands made on them in getting their so-called 'work-life balance' right, the components of their schedule – their all-important social lives, arranging their next holiday jaunt, their gym memberships, and their 'Me-time' – leave precious little time for anything else. Group membership is certainly not a priority for such people.

And, put simply, it is not regarded as *cool*. This might seem a trivial observation, when one can amass so much evidence in support of other socio-economic explanations, the wholesale post-war destruction of local urban communities being just one. But it is the case nevertheless. Part of the counter-cultural ethos of the Sixties and Seventies ruled that membership of established groups meant membership of the establishment itself, which in turn meant stuffiness, petty rituals and – most heinous of all – endorsement of the status quo. Rebellion against this – and against anything that the older generation might have approved of and participated in – became a point of principle. This broadly left-wing response was to come together later in a kind of unholy alliance with the materialist individualism of the Eighties, to produce a toxic mix of infantile self-absorption and status-consciousness in generations for whom the Sixties are not even a distant memory. The end result is now a society which, en masse, dons designer sunglasses – once the symbol of mysterious celebrity, exclusivity and hip rebellion – at the appearance of the very first ray of spring sunshine.

In his impressive work, *Bowling Alone*, the American author Robert Putnam studied the dramatic fall in what he called 'social capital' in the US. He used the popular pastime of bowling as a symbol for a trend that had been similarly marked in that country – a drastic decrease in the numbers of people involved in local, civic and political organisations. He found that, although the level of individuals who bowled had in fact increased by 10 per cent in the years between 1980 and 1993, the number who bowled in leagues had fallen by a massive 40 per cent. He concluded that this social phenomenon, and its resulting deleterious effect on wider civic and physical health, was in part due to the technological individualising effect on society wrought by television and the internet. In a physical sense, this is undeniable: kids who would once have been seen playing on the street in any residential area now immerse themselves in their Gameboys. But people like Harriet would anyway recoil from such an unlikely scene if they came across it in their own street. Like many in our atomised society, they would regard it as all too domestic, too neighbourly, too – well – *provincial* for the life they see themselves living. We talk endlessly now about the importance of 'communities', but this rather masks the fact that there are large numbers of people who actively reject anything that might put them in some sort of context, and that includes neighbourliness.

It is not, therefore, all about the box. But, on a less easily recognisable level, years of exposure to TV and films have arguably led to a subtler change in the way many people see themselves, and consequently in the way they behave.

MY LIFE: THE MOVIE

Like Kayleigh and her mates – whom she would, however, dismiss as major chavs – Harriet and her circle tend to make a production out of their socialising. Bars, cafes and restaurants are now extremely noisy places, as groups compete to show their audience how much fun they're having, and hence how generally successful and 'happening' they are. Listen more closely to the bellowing, and one can hear what often sounds like a script. It's certainly not spontaneous. Laughter is theatrical, forced and unconvincing. The language is hyped: people are *incredible*, events *totally amazing*, this week has invariably been *crazy*. The social dynamic at work seems to have been lifted straight from television shows such as *Friends*, *This Life* or, in the case of Harriet, *Sex and the City*, and one has the sense that these programmes are the yardsticks by which life is unconsciously measured. To be quiet would be ordinary and boring; and that is something to be feared more than death itself.

The mobile phone is crucial in this respect. Despite its ubiquity, using it ostentatiously in a crowded public place still sends out the message: 'I am not here with you drones, I am in demand, I am actually somewhere else.' A request that the caller could perhaps be a little quieter is invariably met with a shocked, indignant response, and a little conspiratorial laugh with the person at the other end, denoting the repressed, general all-round sadness of the complainant. Not just social chitchat, but also conversations of a sometimes excruciatingly personal nature are carried on at full volume – not with any embarrassment or shame, but more for the benefit of those poor souls in immediate proximity who are forced to suffer it. And when the narrative finally finishes, on goes the iPod, and the individual is again absent from his or her physical surroundings.

In the narcissistic spirit of our age, it's all about letting others be damned. 'You should get out more' is one of Harriet's favourite current put-downs, but maybe the best option really is to stay in with your books and CDs; or, horror of horrors, follow the hobby or interest you keep to yourself so as to avoid the general mockery of others. Either that, or run the risk of feeling genuinely homicidal by the end of a day of ordinary human activities, such as work, travel and an evening out. As far as anti-social behaviour goes, the selfishness of others encountered on a daily basis is hardly ASBO material. What it does show is a belief in the supremacy of the importance of self over the comfort and feeling of others, and it cuts across all social groups and milieu, including, of course, Harriet's. The actor Kevin Spacey, installed a few years back as artistic director of the Old Vic, recently railed against the ever-growing chorus of ring tones during theatre performances. 'My feeling is if people don't know how to behave, they shouldn't come', he declared courageously. He'd already shown the strength of his feelings about this by snapping 'Tell them we're busy!' when a phone went off while he was on stage during *The Iceman Cometh*. Similarly, the actor Richard Griffiths went so far as to stop a recent performance of *The History Boys* at the National Theatre, exasperated at the persistent beeping of a pager. 'I'm sorry, but I can't compete with your electronic device', he declared to the mortification of the culprit.

Even the expression of appreciation of, say, a live performance has become a matter of drawing attention to, and saying something about, yourself. Those who have shown every sign of utter boredom (such as sleeping) during a ballet or opera rally themselves enough to whoop like demented hyenas on a TV game show when the curtain comes down. This imported practice makes the self-centred feel part of the artistic process – you've had your moment, they're saying, now I'll have mine.

'Is it another mark of the Me generation?' wrote Arlene Croce in the *New Yorker* when this whooping was first heard on the American scene years ago. 'All the traditional audience vocables – Bravos, oles – say "You were wonderful"; they're directed to the performer. These wordless woofs say, "I'm wiped out."' Croce was spot on: perhaps old-fashioned clapping is just too – well – altruistic.

YOU'RE WORTH IT

If, like Harriet, you don't 'do' neighbours, then there's hardly any point in keeping up with the Joneses. In fact, that old saying, with its implied assumption that what the Joneses possessed, thought or did was actually of some consequence, has rather a quaint, nostalgic feel to it.

Now, many of us set our sights rather higher. Celebrities have become the benchmark for those who take their cue, along with any sense of communal feeling that they might possess, from the TV and its relentless stream of lifestyle makeover programmes. What you buy is increasingly seen as an expression of yourself. Ask any marketing man, and he will tell you that most consumers fall into certain familiar categories, and that, in terms of their desires, responses and tastes, the differences between people are far, far smaller than the striking and often predictable similarities. But this is no longer something that people feel very happy about accepting.

Take two recent magazine advertisements, designed with polar opposite ends of the market place in mind, but both containing the same message. The first would find more of an audience with Kayleigh and her friends. It is for a hamburger chain, and has the legend 'Have it Your Way' emblazoned above the copy, which states boldly:

> You have the right to have what you want, exactly when you want it. Because on the menu of life, you are 'Today's Special'.

The other ad is for so-called designer luggage, and might appeal to Harriet. A picture of a rather ugly-looking case, of the fashionable sort, with wheels and a handle, is framed against the sea, out of which the fashionista Alexander McQueen is emerging, wet-shirted and expressionless. 'Escape the Ordinary' runs the caption.

As with the intensely irritating beauty-product TV commercials which fawn 'You're worth it' – or, even worse, 'I'm worth it' – in both of these ads it's all about Me. Flattering the sense of individuality of the customer has always been a part of advertising, but for much of its life it was an industry constrained by the need to send one punchy, catch-all line to a mass market. This has changed dramatically in the past decade, especially as technological changes have allowed product marketing to become more easily and specifically targeted. The underlying message, whether applied to burgers, bags or banks, is not so much the traditional one – that this product will help make you sexier or cooler, with its implication that, in a way, we are all in this together – but rather that you are special, that your needs are special, that we've realised this and we can provide what you uniquely require.

Professor Jean Twenge, an American academic and writer, noticed this trend in her own country a few years ago. In *Generation Me: Why Today's Young Americans Are More Confident, Assertive, Entitled – and More Miserable Than Ever Before*, she describes how the insurance company Prudential replaced its longstanding slogan 'Get a Piece of the Rock' with 'Be Your Own Rock', and, amazingly, how the US Army has adopted the slogan 'An Army of One'.

Twenge writes that marketing men have simply spotted, and responded to, ways in which everyday language has been hijacked by the Self. On the book's website she lists some examples of these everyday sayings, worth reproducing here, as they can be heard just as commonly in Clapham as in Connecticut:

- Worried about how to act in a social situation? 'Just be yourself.'
- What's the good thing about your alcoholism/drug addiction/murder conviction? 'I learned a lot about myself.'
- Concerned about your performance? 'Believe in yourself.' (Often followed by 'and anything is possible'.)
- Should you buy the new pair of shoes or get the nose ring? 'Yes, express yourself.'
- Why should you leave the unfulfilling relationship/quit the boring job/tell off your mother-in-law? 'You have to respect yourself.'
- Trying to get rid of a bad habit? 'Be honest with yourself.'
- Confused about the best time to date or get married? 'You have to love yourself before you can love someone else.'
- Should you express your opinion? 'Yes, stand up for yourself.'

'Today's college students are more likely to have a feeling of self-importance, to be entitled, and in general, to be more narcissistic', says Twenge. 'About two-thirds of current college students score above-average on narcissism, and that's 30% more than in 1982.'

However, Harriet would be so used to using and hearing statements like those above that she would be goggle-eyed at the sheer sadness of somebody who took them at anything other than face value.

SHRINK-WRAPPED

My own experience of living in California – admittedly the most privatised, celebrity-fixated, self-loving state in the US – yielded some nice, juicy examples of Twenge's list. I once attended the funeral service of an artist acquaintance, which was held, in the true spirit of 'spirituality', on the beach at Santa Monica. Nobody wore black, of course: way too traditional and anti-individualistic. Oration followed oration – such informality tends to lead to verbosity – and the person who bulked largest at the gathering was usually the one speaking at any given time. As we walked away at sunset, a friend reflected quietly on the event. 'It was wonderful. So moving. A real growing moment for me', he said. 'It made me feel so calm, so amazingly at peace with myself.'

This particular guy put a great emphasis on nurturing his spiritual side. Harriet is the same; she might laugh incredulously when her date hints at church-going, because, of course, as everybody knows, organised religion is a total fraud. Instead, she looks at what is best for her and her unique needs. She is, after all, at the centre of the universe, so this is the only practical way to see to her inner self. So yoga has its role in keeping her focused and in touch with herself, astrology is a bit of harmless fun and is actually, she's found, surprisingly accurate (she's a typical Aquarian). And her gap-year trip to Ghana, during which she'd been an assistant teacher at a village school, taught her quite how much it was possible to grow spiritually through the experience of helping others.

She also nourishes herself with the occasional bout of therapy – some Me-time with herself. The outside world barely exists on these occasions, although external events, if big enough, can intrude: the death of Diana caused much soul-searching, apparently, among female therapy patients. Researching a newspaper article in LA on how people at a local level had reacted to 9/11, I asked a therapist, Dr Morgan, to describe the reaction of her clients. Some had felt it had put their problems in context – which, although being oddly narcissistic in a way, was, I suppose, acceptable in its banality. Others, however, had no such inhibitions. 'Some patients have related it totally to their own problems', she said. 'After September 11th, one said he was glad that other people would now know what it was like for him growing up, being terrorised by his family.' Such breathtaking self-absorption perhaps comes at the extreme end of the spectrum; but I wager that, if he had said this at a social gathering instead of to a shrink, nobody would have pulled him up on it. It would be seen, in today's oddly rearranged universe, as a sign of his sensitivity, of somebody who was evolving and 'brave' enough to be in touch with his inner self.

Therapy is one of the biggest growth industries in the UK. Counsellors are the new secular clergy, with the marvellously named 'life coaches' their altar boys. The language of the session has infiltrated everyday speech, even political discourse, and we can all talk about 'closure' now, while still not really knowing what it entails. In fact, very recent evidence has confirmed the belief of the World War II generation that some sort of activity, even just walking in the fresh air, is probably the best way of lessening anxiety and depression. Such a simple piece of homespun wisdom was always greeted with much impatient irritation by the baby boomers, many of whom had become fascinated with their own internal contradictions and problems, and possibly didn't even want them solved. And besides, a brisk walk doesn't involve an audience of any kind.

After 9/11, it was a relief when a comic actor friend, one of the old showbiz school, had the grace to be self-mocking. I asked him whether, during his own therapeutic activity, he would now be looking outwards to the world more often. 'It depends', he answered. 'Will it cost more?'

IS NARCISSISM ON THE INCREASE, OR IS IT JUST ME?

With their traditionally tolerated self-absorption and highly valued, allegedly unique insights, the artists among us have always been able to play the narcissism card and get away with it. Tracey Emin can be celebrated – by critics at least – for her famously self-referential tent installation 'Everyone I Have Ever Slept With, 1963–1995', and then, when asked on David Frost's TV show why this should be considered art, for answering 'Because I say it is'.

At the same time, national newspapers, especially the supposedly serious broadsheets, have never been so clogged up with personal columns in which commentators offer vignettes of their everyday lives, usually accompanied by observations of quite astounding banality. This trend reached a new peak recently when two such writers treated readers of one paper to a blow-by-blow account of the breakdown of their marriage. Since they could not be considered celebrities in even the most debased sense, one wonders who the hell was interested. The satirical magazine *Private Eye* carries a regular spoof of such this-and-that columns, written by the appositely named Polly Filler, although much of this stuff is already beyond parody.

Harriet and the thousands like her, who might consider Tracey cool and don't see a problem with Polly, don't want to be left behind; they've been weaned on the belief that they have their own infinite creativity, their own unique needs and desires, which have simply yet to find an outlet, a worthy partner, or proper recognition. Such self-centredness can play havoc, especially on the romance front. The shelves groan with paperbacks offering formulas for finding the right partner; or, if you are stuck with the wrong one, how to make him or her into love's young dream. Or for the even more ambitious there is advice on how to detect your soul mate – a doomed exercise, perhaps, if one is starting from a position of splendid, self-loving isolation.

Much that has been written in recent years about the cult of narcissism holds it to be proof of our society's decadence. Blame in small or large degree has been laid at the door of a capitalist system run rampant. For example, writing in the *New Statesman* with a forthcoming Valentine's Day in mind, Neil Clark quoted from Erich Fromm's book, *The Art of Loving*, in which Fromm considered 'if the social structure of Western civilisation and the spirit arising from it are conducive to the development of love' and concluded that 'to raise the question is to answer it in the negative'. Clark went on to comment that:

> ... a society that is driven by rapacious commercialism, which lauds and promotes the cult of self, and which quantifies success in purely material terms, will always produce less love and therefore more unhappy people than one which places human needs first. Global capitalism does many things, but building solidarity is not among them.

There is something in this, but the problem with such an approach is that it ignores the results of the decades of critiquing and undermining of traditional institutions which had hitherto given people a sense of context and belonging. We will go into this in greater depth later on, but suffice it to say that, so far as relationships are concerned, many people seem to have taken to heart Cyril Connolly's comment that the pram in the hallway is the enemy of creativity – and, he could have added, the enemy of the untrammelled realisation of the glorious self.

For some, this realisation comes in the transformation of the body. Men, in particular, have grown far more conscious of their sexuality, in the sense that they see it as something to parade and accentuate – quite happy, it seems, to effectively objectify themselves. As the need for strength for manual work has drastically declined, so the development of a powerful muscular physique, to be used for decorative purposes, has become more common. Indeed, the use of that very word – physique – now has a quaint ring to it. Safely un-sexual, it could be used by one man commenting on the attributes of another. It has largely been replaced by 'body' – and 'he has a great body' has a far more sexual ring to it than 'he has an excellent physique'.

The way in which gay culture has become part of the mainstream must have had an effect here, as must the far less inhibited reporting over the past few decades of what women find attractive. The overall result has been the emergence of a man who takes pleasure in ostentatiously showing off his biceps, waxed torso and cute behind, fully conscious of the effect it might have; in another era, he would have expended as much energy on cultivating traditional (and fully clothed) male pulls, such as strength, power and wealth.

In the mid Nineties, the journalist Mark Simpson came to call such men 'metrosexuals'. They could be straight, gay or bisexual, or happily cultivate the image of fluid sexuality, and be perfectly happy receiving the adoration of both sexes. As the writer Simon Crompton has pointed out in his book, *All About Me – Loving a Narcissist*, one has only to look at the actors who have been chosen to play James Bond to see how times have changed in this respect: in the early Sixties, it was Sean Connery, a hairy former milkman, who fitted the role; while the latest incumbent, Daniel Craig, is a blond, smooth, self-consciously super-muscular type who could just as easily have stepped out of a gay porn movie. He doesn't so much move as position himself. As he emerges from the sea in that now famous scene, the body is almost shouting *Look at me!* It could also be whispering *...but don't touch!*, for physical self-obsession is probably more of a barrier to spontaneous feeling and altruistic instincts than the more commonly blamed emotional variety.

In this general climate, then, it is hardly surprising if, for people like Harriet, the dating game has taken on the air of the showbiz audition. Each participant has his or her mental checklist. Expectations are based all too often on each individual's self-evaluation. The mentality of the curriculum vitae is applied as rigorously as in the employment arena. The new practice of speed-dating is a completely realistic evolution of this; it is effectively the first-round interview, during which those judged inadequate can be weeded out.

However, when it finally comes to taking the plunge, putting on a show for others is the order of the day. Just as the very point of them is being gradually abandoned, weddings have become increasingly lavish mini-productions, with the happy couple playing the role of leading man and leading lady. Few who embark on marriage might even countenance the thought that this thing is traditionally meant to be for keeps; if your life is a movie, then it has to have its set pieces, its dramatic climaxes and its cliff-hangers. And these come at a price: the average amount spent on a wedding is now a staggering £18,000 (not including all the presents, of course). As the journalist Andrew O'Hagan put it in the *Daily Telegraph*, they have become somewhat grotesque orgies of spending:

> ...to go by the antics of the average young British couple, you'd think the decision to get married was akin to the inauguration of an election campaign or the sending of a Task Force to the Falklands: noisy, hysterical, with lots of sickness, no certainty of success, and the promise of vast expense on every front.

I CLICK, THEREFORE I AM

If the prospect of all this simply gets too much, you can always retreat into your own private world. Not necessarily of the old-fashioned, Billy Liar, day-dreaming variety, for things have moved on somewhat. If you feel overlooked in this life, there is no need to go and shoot up your local primary school; thanks to the internet, you can now completely reinvent yourself, or become a web celeb, with thousands of unseen friends or fans, at the click of a mouse. In recent years, networking websites have grown exponentially: MySpace has well over 100 million members, and Facebook – a kind of mixture of email and personal profile – has nearly 30 million. These sites have spawned a whole new branch of personality cult, most of which is dedicated to self-promotion of one kind or another, although they also throw up the odd, harmlessly obscure character who then finds himself with a massive audience. Peter Oakley, an 80-year-old widower, posted a video of himself simply talking about his life on YouTube in 2006. A year on, his clip had registered 2.65 million views. So it is appropriate that, at a time when web content is increasingly being controlled by consumers using it to project themselves, *Time* magazine's Person of the Year in 2006 was You.

It is but a small step from this to Second Life, the most famous of a host of virtual worlds which have seen a similar growth. The creation of Philip Rosedale, a 28-year-old internet entrepreneur who was inspired by Neal Stephenson's sci-fi novel *Snow Crash*, Second Life offers a complete existence to those for whom, presumably, reality is just not working out. It has its own companies, currency, banks, landscape and accommodation.

Real fortunes can be made. Reuters has its own beat reporter there. The individual user can create a completely new alter ego, called an 'avatar', which can range from an idealised version of oneself (leading to an awful lot of Lara Crofts) to some fantastically buff superhero Warrior of the Un-dead type. But Second Life is not just some adolescent video playground – this is grown-up stuff.

The sky (or at least the boundaries of commerce) is surely the limit with such ventures. Nobody need ever be ordinary again. If, as is happening, the money-making potential and social importance of such virtual worlds is taken more and more seriously, we might arrive at a situation where real talent, or distinction, or even natural physical beauty, loses all value. We will have divested ourselves of all context, while at the same time fooling ourselves that, by creating an illusory version of ourselves, we are taking part in a wonderfully creative act of individual imagination. It's a horrible prospect. Dating, however, should certainly be easier.

CHAPTER FIVE

MARC & SUE'S WORLD

Everyone wants to save the world. No one wants
to help Mom do the dishes.

P. J. O'Rourke

Was there ever a grander title than Citizen of the World? Was there ever a moniker, when self-ascribed, more likely to stop criticism in its tracks? How can one argue with the all-embracing inclusiveness, the moral rectitude, the sheer individual expansiveness implicit in its claim? Why, those who call themselves a citizen of France, a British subject or a Glaswegian first and foremost, should consider themselves properly stunted when confronted with such a majestic state of self-realisation. It's enough to make you feel un-evolved.

Undaunted by (and maybe even ignorant of) the experiences of women and gay men in Islamic states, by the extent of human rights abuses in China, by the total physical and mental tyranny practised in North Korea, and by the sexual use of babies as a cure for HIV in Africa, the Citizens of the World march on, cherry-picking as they go from the global kaleidoscope of cultures, distinguishing themselves by their rejection of the petty concerns of those somewhat closer to home, existing on a special plane far removed from such parochialism.

They have no roots – or at least, they have endeavoured to set themselves free of such constraining influences. Local charities, therefore, do not interest them much; although they are, of course, fully behind the big, ostentatious, global fund drives, especially ones like Live 8 or Live Earth, with their strong whiff of self-blame and anti-Americanism. They see themselves existing happily anywhere in the world – or at least in the bits of it they've seen on one of their several annual holidays or countless work trips. They pride themselves on bringing a bit of Tokyo, or Laos or New York back to their existence here, imbuing it with shades of cosmopolitan knowingness – although, truth be told, they have become rather *concerned* about the effect on the environment of cheap air travel and of the millions who can now follow in their wake.

Like many urban, professional types of the 21st century, marketing supremo Marc and his TV exec partner Sue tend to think of themselves as Citizens of the World (although, as members of the media class, their finely honed irony radar stops them from using the rather corny phrase itself). Of course, unlike hoi polloi, they have come to all their conclusions about the world – which are mostly left-leaning – through their own, unique mental processes. They have developed their tastes independently of outside influences. As sophisticated people, they are acutely aware of the unique needs, likes and dislikes of their minds and bodies, and wish that others took as much care as they do. They are resolutely averse to being part of the crowd, they are emphatically not part of any tradition; and the taste that Marc has developed for football in the past decade is more about a desire to experience the masculine side of his character than about any ridiculous sense of geographic or national tribalism.

Their own sense of moral purity dictates how they feel about events and issues. The self-regarding placards that they carried at the anti-Iraq War demonstration a few years back – 'Not in My Name!' – suited them down to the ground. The fact that they were then marching behind people whose views would have struck them, if they had considered them rationally (or even known about them), as illiberal to say the least, was neither here nor there. This was about Marc & Sue, and how and what they thought of themselves. The experience left them almost high.

The couple and their friends have made London their own, and the capital is starting to resemble New York in its separation from the country as a whole. In *The Times*, the columnist Gerard Baker got it right:

> London's political culture has been uprooted from its English heritage. It is run – if you can call it that – by a sort of post-modern communist Mayor, whose political voice – minus the annoying nasal whine – would sound right at home in Paris, Bologna or San Francisco. It hosts a metropolitan elite that loftily gazes three ways: outward, at the supposed superiority of anything not British; inward, at its own ineffable genius; and down its elegantly pampered nose, at the provincial trivialities that consume the dreary lives of the rest of the population.

Marc & Sue would be horrified at the suggestion that they had anything in common with Kayleigh and her chavvy shenanigans, or even Harriet and her addiction to hyperbole. They are above all this, of course. But in their own smug, immaculately organic way, their struggle to be special is every bit as intense.

WE ARE ALL BOHEMIANS NOW

It was easier to rebel against the expectations of family, class or nation when conventions were strictly imposed. But now, breaking the rules – whether imagined or real – has become the rule itself. There is, for example, little transgressive shock value to be had in recreational drug-taking when over two million people do it on a regular weekly basis.

As the writer Theodore Dalrymple observed in the *Guardian* when describing those demi-gods of Bohemia, the Bloomsbury group:

> In a demotic age...their justification for personal license could not long be confined to socially superior types such as themselves. Before very long, what was permissible for the elite became mandatory for hoi

polloi; and when the predictable social disaster occurred, in the form of a growing underclass devoid of moral bearings, the elite that had absorbed (indeed, revelled in) Bloomsbury's influence took the growth of the underclass as evidence that their original grudge against society and its conventions had been justified all along. The philosophy brought about the disaster, and the disaster justified the philosophy.

Living in a state of permanent counter-cultural rebellion might flatter the individual's desire to see him or herself as being outside the norm, but unfortunately for the likes of Marc & Sue, it has become as stiflingly predictable as anything supposedly endured by past generations. The fact that the dreary annual pilgrimage to the Glastonbury music festival is written up in *The Times* as virtually part of the social season – appearing as inevitably as a wet Wimbledon – is just one case in point.

Still, there is always one's communion with and understanding of The Other to help mark one out. The Other comes in all shapes and sizes; but the point is to support it on principle, wherever it may pop up, as a way of distinguishing oneself from the majority or the mainstream. Artists who 'break boundaries', however inept or talentless they might be, and however non-existent the boundaries, are to be feted. Whether or not you think that the sculpture of 'Alison Lapper Pregnant' in Trafalgar Square is a crashingly mediocre piece of art (and in your heart of hearts you probably do), it is nevertheless to be praised for the way in which it fearlessly holds the rest of us to account for our allegedly retarded attitude towards the disabled. If asked to choose between the formal garden plan or the randomly chaotic, the randomly chaotic will, naturally, be preferred. Ethnic tribal ceremonial masks will always take precedence over the Apollo Belvedere. The long-winded, self-conscious independent film will always trump the Hollywood movie, the quirky-looking art-house actor automatically given credibility denied the regularly handsome box-office star. Edgy camera work will always be proclaimed more truthful than the conventional shot. Jeans are naturally to be trusted over suits. Other cultures will have more intrinsic value than one's own. The West will always be treated with hostility, shame or scepticism, the motives of its possible enemies as benign. Black is always right; white invariably wrong. New equals good; old equals bad. And so on and so forth.

Some will easily recognise the approach underlying all of these attitudes as that of traditional Guardianistas – which, indeed, is what most of the people who embody them are. The access to opinion-forming enjoyed by this group has meant that such views have had a hugely disproportionate cultural influence. This, along with the gradual process of 'embourgeoisement' of recent decades has meant that this way of looking at things has spread further than the confines of Hampstead and Islington, to those who now know little of their culture or history but might like to see themselves as suitably thoughtful, nuanced, and above all *modern*. A little learning is a corrosive, if not necessarily a dangerous, thing.

SMIRKERS OF THE WORLD UNITE

Majority or mainstream tastes that would otherwise be beneath contempt can still be enjoyed, of course; but this must be done strictly between invisible quote marks. Even Marc's recent trips to Arsenal's terraces have a little self-referential ironic tinge. Irony has become so feted over the past decade or so that it would seem to have developed a virtual stranglehold on our culture.

Implicit in it, of course, is a sense of defeat and hopelessness. But that hasn't stopped it becoming the benchmark for contemporary sophistication. Knowing whether a musical, a concert by the Bee Gees or a repeat of *I Love Lucy* is to be enjoyed ironically or not marks one out – not just from the poor, ordinary souls who, in all innocence, might actually be finding these things entertaining, but also for one's good taste and general intellectual awareness. You will still be one of the seven million or so who contribute to the ratings hit for the latest piece of popular reality TV, but you can comfort yourself with the knowledge that, unlike the great unwashed watching, you have arrived at this via *a completely different route*.

Being nicely ironic is the most wonderfully effective defence against accusations of populism or reactionary-ism. It can protect you against friends' disapproval at a badly chosen piece of furniture, or a liking for Chicken Kiev. It means you can have a fondue dinner party or an avocado and prawn starter, or get a lump in your throat watching the Last Night of the Proms, without having to be ashamed or considered naff. It also means you can laugh heartily at the latest faddish comedian's jokes about wheelchairs and women, comfortable in the knowledge that nobody will mistake you for a Bernard Manning fan.

As the journalist Zoe Williams explained in the *Guardian*:

> [O]ther strands of media use irony to assert their right to have no position whatsoever. So, you take a cover of FHM, with tits on the front – and it's ironic because it appears to be saying 'women are objects', yet of course it isn't saying that, because we're in a postfeminist age. But nor is it saying 'women aren't objects', because that would be dated, over-sincere, mawkish even. So, it's effectively saying 'women are neither objects, nor non-objects – and here are some tits!' *Scary Movie 2*, *Dumb And Dumberer*, posh women who go to pole-dancing classes, people who set the video for *Big Brother Live*, people who have Eurovision Song Contest evenings, *Charlie's Angels* (the film, not the TV series) and about a million other things besides, are all using this ludic trope – 'I'm not saying what you think I'm saying, but I'm not saying its opposite, either. In fact, I'm not saying anything at all. But I get to keep the tits.'

Being ironic means having your cake and eating it, while also remaining smugly above the crowd. Unfortunately, it also kills stone dead the expression of anything resembling genuine enthusiasm – unless, of course, it is for that which is deemed transgressive, subversive, or otherwise not of the majority. After all, Marc & Sue would never dream of giving black culture, or 'Alison Lapper Pregnant', the irony treatment.

MINORITY INTERESTS

In fact, minorities are always singled out for special treatment in Marc & Sue's world, which is to say that they are virtually beyond criticism. Understanding and celebrating them is an expression of the couple's unique broadmindedness, moral character and cosmopolitanism. Sue's complaint that, while the area they live in is great, it is also really rather *white*, is evidence not of her inverse racism (she would never, of course, complain about Brixton being really rather black) but of her multi-facetedness, and her rejection of stifling conformity.

As many even on the traditional Left would now agree, the disastrous effects of the liberal metropolitan elite's espousal and promotion of multiculturalism at all costs are becoming clearer by the day – especially now that the policy is coming apart at the seams. They are coming to see, rather late in the day, the contradictions in their beloved doctrine (although for many of them these contradictions still remain at the stage of dinner party discussion points and the odd newspaper column). There is no space here to go into a full consideration of what is one of the most important issues facing the country; suffice it to say that the social effects of encouraging ethnic minorities to nurse a grievance culture based on perceived wrongs, which is then reconfirmed at every opportunity – and always with reference to the innately racist, bigoted, unthinking majority – are looming increasingly large in mainstream political discourse.

The granting of such special status has led to a form of immunity from even the mildest criticism. This protection mostly takes the form of shielding such special-interest groups from being offended by others – whether it be by a comedian's joke, a simple look in the street, or the publication of a set of satirical cartoons. When the capacity for taking offence is seemingly limitless, it is hardly surprising if most people come to the conclusion that it is easier, if not actually safer, to say nothing at all; which pretty much sums up the situation as it currently stands in Britain.

The problems really start when offence is taken at your very existence – or at least at how you choose to live your life. Marc & Sue are slowly catching up on all of this; but, for the time being at least, they are managing to stick to their line by not thinking too much about honour killings, burkas and what many Muslims might think of some of the arty gay friends they have to dinner on a regular basis.

WITH MINIMALIST EFFORT

Rarely will their parents be at such gatherings. The couple have rather kicked over their traces, so far as their suburban backgrounds are concerned, and, along with their friends, despise grammar schools of the sort that got Sue into Oxbridge, not to mention the kind of minor public school that Marc attended. They cringe at their parents' *Daily Mail* sensibilities – but really, what can you expect? That generation doesn't know any better, and anyway, they'll be dying out soon.

In the meantime, their other guests will be entertained amid immaculately minimalist surroundings: gleaming white walls, grey tiled floors, sparkling and empty surfaces, and everything packed away in sets of drawers that can only be located by touch – all of which tends to transform guests who are given the obligatory tour into members of a blindness-empathy class. The overall effect is of a carefully crafted stage set, designed to throw the occupants into sharp relief, liberated from anything so constraining as a context. The bareness is proclaiming: 'We do not need to display our personalities about us. You will not find out about us from something as mundane as looking at our bookshelves. We are endlessly fascinating, and we present ourselves to you whole, unfettered by the collected clutter of experience.'

The fashion for such minimalist interiors first took hold in the Eighties, soon spreading to restaurants, shops and hotels, all of which spent hundreds of thousands on creating a sense of nothingness, which at the same time turned the spotlight on the individuals who were invited to move about in it ('suspended in time and space', as London's achingly minimalist boutique hotel The Hempel puts it). Of course, like all displays of pomposity and self-importance, the bubble is easily pricked. A single sweet wrapper on a lobby floor can throw the whole fragile enterprise seriously out of kilter. Edwardian grandeur, on the other hand, is altogether more outward looking and forgiving of the odd bit of untidiness; its unapologetic exuberance probably makes more self-absorbed souls feel uncomfortable and – the worst crime of all – ignored.

In the late Nineties, I made a documentary for Channel 4 about the then new lifestyle magazine *Wallpaper**. At that time (I think it has changed somewhat since) it was a publication that was devoted to cool modernism in all its forms, setting its sights on a readership of urban dwellers who, as its founder Tyler Brûlé pointed out to us, had more in common – or aspired to have more in common – with their counterparts in New York and Tokyo than, as he charmingly put it, 'someone in a trailer park in Staines'. As a result, most of the interiors it depicted looked like hotel rooms. It flattered those who saw themselves as the new international elite (London's *Evening Standard* recently gave them their own tribal label – 'Globos'), had a nice touch in chaste homoeroticism (many of its readers would, after all, have been metrosexuals) and an (inevitably) ironic tongue in its cheek. It was all about adopting styles which proclaimed something about you, the reader, and where you saw yourself in a world that was your oyster.

This urge to de-contextualise has made its way back to the dreaded suburbs, albeit unconsciously. The increasing concreting over of front gardens, and the 'decking' of back ones, is, on the face of it, a response to growing parking problems – and maybe an increased awareness of *Neighbours*-style

Australian barbecue living. But it also carries with it more than a hint of the paving over of roots, and an aspirational desire not to be of this setting. The paring down of interiors has also seeped past the net curtains and into the front living room, and now sits uncomfortably inside many a half-timbered exterior.

There's a downside to the creation of so many personal temples. A few years back, a BBC documentary rather amusingly showed how, having spent fortunes creating their Teflon habitats, the pioneers of minimalism were forced to shave off all those cutting-edge, potentially lethal corners the minute crawling babies showed up on the scene. This is something Marc & Sue will have to face up to soon, as Sue is expecting the now customary one child – at the obligatory age of 41.

DOES MY BRAIN LOOK BIG IN THIS?

If there's one thing we know for certain that people have been doing since time began, it's having children. But for many women in Sue's milieu, giving birth will be treated as the celebration of a unique talent – for those lucky enough to witness it, the most wonderful thing that they are ever likely to see. In the coming years, the child will be neurotically tended, over-protected, praised and congratulated as though it were a little piece of art, a work in progress. Sue's mother really cannot see what all the fuss is about, but has learned the hard way to shut up about it.

Sue is fiercely proud of being pregnant, and so wears one of those cropped, skin-tight T-shirts that are designed to show off her stomach in all its bare glory. She wants people to see and to know that she has no intention of hiding her new creation under the kind of voluminous maternity garb her mother's generation would have worn. When confronted with it in public, many people (she senses) tend to avert their eyes from her massive midriff – which, in her view, shows just how many repressive, outmoded attitudes there still are around.

Column inches about new trends in tie-less Tories notwithstanding, the more fundamental question of what has happened to the way people dress is rarely commented on, perhaps because to complain about the way we present ourselves to each other in contemporary society runs the risk of marking one out as an unreconstructed buffer of the old school, and thus a bit of a joke. Taking the view that Sue really isn't the first woman to have a baby, and so needn't proclaim the feat to all and sundry, would be seen at best as the mark of a reactionary misogynist; at worst as an attack on her liberty of the individual.

The belief that you should 'express yourself' through what you wear is a relatively new one, very much part and parcel of the values of the Me Generation identified by Tom Wolfe in the Seventies and the counter-culture of the decade that preceded it. Expressing your own individual sense of style, or dressing in what makes you happiest and most comfortable, regardless of the context, is the unchallengeable criterion now. You can cover yourself with tattoos, pierce your eyebrows and belly button and wear T-shirts with lame slogans ('Do I Look Like I'm Interested?') which are designed to alienate others and simultaneously draw attention to aspects of your character you have decided are interesting.

But all this misses the point of what dressing with a degree of smartness – or at least in something appropriate for the occasion – was all about. The instinct not to attend a funeral in jeans, or a wedding in shorts and trainers, came not (or not necessarily) from an innate preference for suits or ties, or from a slavish desire to uphold convention, but from a sense of consideration and respect for others. Unshined shoes, the *Vogue* editor Diana Vreeland famously said, are the end of civilisation. It followed that the way in which you appeared said as much about what you thought of those around you as it did about what you thought of yourself. If you have been encouraged not to care what others think – or, as is increasingly the case, not even to be aware of those around you – then it is hard to see why you should give a damn (one wonders what Vreeland would have made of the virtual death, in some parts of the western world, of the shoe itself). Such a lack of consideration or effort, with its implicit selfishness, has a demoralising, energy-sapping and generally lowering effect on public life. Few will admit to this, but it is something that is borne out by the widespread nostalgia for the often more formal fashions of even the quite recent past that now cuts across all generations.

Dressing well went hand in hand with a strong sense of collective identity, particularly among the traditional working class. This has been misunderstood by generations of middle-class interferers, who rather arrogantly assumed that they were imposing their own bourgeois standards on the workers, who should be freed from such restrictions. I remember, as a first-generation college boy from a working-class family, in the late Seventies being confronted with Trotskyite public schoolboys who, in their desperate attempt to appear down with us proles, took to swearing a lot at Union meetings, not shaving, and dressing as slobbily as possible. They were completely misguided if they thought this was what being working class meant, of course – as well as being outrageously insulting.

But somehow they won the day: over the past 30 years, the working class has indeed transformed itself into something it never was, and is now fully living up to the middle-class view of it. The result is an army of what we might call 'kidults', who can be seen in any high street or shopping mall: chubby middle-aged men in long shorts, baggy slogan-covered tops and trainers, waddling like huge babies, clasping bottles of water topped off with those special drinking teats. And they make up the one minority group about which Marc & Sue can be condescending while feeling totally at ease.

Furthermore, self-absorption can lead to odd clothing choices, which defy even the need to be comfortable at all costs. An old school friend of mine, certainly not a Bufton Tufton, who was visiting London from his home in Italy, was mystified to see commuters standing on the railway station in just T-shirts or cardigans in the middle of a harsh winter. He could not have imagined seeing the same in his adopted country. He concluded that this was the behaviour of people who had become completely detached from their environment, and indeed from their very climate. The outside world had little bearing on how they lived their lives or on the choices they made. They would undoubtedly be pleased to hear this, even as they were shivering. And with their dread of conformity, Marc & Sue would applaud their decision not to wrap up warmly.

CHAPTER SIX

JASON'S WORLD

Time and time again up until his death, Jessie humiliated the gangsters to their face by saying no to the gang.

Barbara Reid, mother of murdered teenager Jessie James

A survey published in 2007 revealed that nearly 1.1 million people in the UK are now claiming they cannot work and are living on incapacity benefit as a result of 'mental disorders and behavioural problems'. This reveals a massive rise in just under a decade – up 49 per cent from a figure of 732,100 in 1997. Claimants range from people categorised as suffering from 'severe stress' through to those with 'personality disorders', but they also include individuals with 'eating disorders' (1,830), unspecified 'mood disorders' (5,770) and the vaguely named 'other anxiety disorders' (115,850). By far the biggest single group is made up of those rendered economically inactive due to 'depressive episodes' – a whopping 501,520.

Young Jason is one of these. Much of his depression is brought on by his particular and deeply entrenched 'issues' with self-esteem, i.e. he has none. Or rather, this is what he's heard countless times from the counsellor he was assigned to, and from people like him he's seen on Jeremy Kyle's daytime talk show. The constant peddling of this pop psychology, and the quick, easy line in explanation it affords, means that even his Mum and Dad feel the pressure to abandon their misgivings and go along with it. He can't stick at anything, has a problem with authority, and feels utterly misunderstood. He swears he tries his best, but everywhere his efforts are thwarted.

However, Jason has been the victim of an incorrect diagnosis. He has, in fact, entrenched issues with self-pity. This is something he does indeed have plenty of, and, rather than any 'depressive episodes', this is what weighs him down. Depression is an increasingly elastic term: more than 31 million prescriptions for anti-depressants were issued in England in early 2007, a record high, and a rise of 6 per cent in just two years.

As Professor Gordon Parker has pointed out in the *British Medical Journal*, too many people are being diagnosed with depression when, in fact, they are merely unhappy. There is, he wrote, too low a threshold for clinical depression, which means that quite ordinary emotional states can be classified as an illness. 'Over the last 30 years the formal definitions for defining clinical depression have expanded into the territory of normal depression,' he wrote, 'and the real risk is that the milder, more common experiences risk being pathologised.'

This is in line with the increasing tendency to promote everyday nuisances, behavioural ticks and otherwise ordinary, often self-destructive, behaviour into a series of -ologies and -isms, as BT's Beattie might have put it. As well as shifting responsibility from the individual, having a recognised medical condition attributed to one is, after all, so much more *interesting*. Addictions of all colours – including to sex – have, over recent decades, been reclassified as illnesses, thus entirely negating the crucial element of personal autonomy inherent in the word 'addiction'. Allergies are multiplying, as are 'intolerances' to this and that (although not everyone is convinced: as the American comedian Chris Rock joked, 'Hungry people ain't allergic to shit. You think anyone in Rwanda's got a fuckin' lactose intolerance?!'). But which is really more likely – a genuine, sudden surge in a condition called Attention Deficit Disorder (ADD) in small kids, which then has to be treated with sedative drugs, or an alarming trend among parents and schools to leave naturally boisterous and anarchic young kids totally undisciplined?

Anyway, being prone to depression is fine with Jason. In what he thinks are some of his more lucid moments – usually when he's arguing with his parents about getting a job – he claims that if *he* were an employer, *he* wouldn't employ him. He preens over this manipulative insight, presenting it as an example of his self-knowledge, which his well-meaning parents then find hard to counter. He's obviously an intelligent kid, they reason, and they don't live on some sink estate, so maybe it really is the case that he's one of life's misfits – an outsider, too sensitive for his own good, a natural rebel. Jason's comfortable with this analysis, as he is with blaming his crap teachers for failing to ensure that he reached the enormous potential they kept talking about. It was, after all, his right to achieve the recognition that he felt was his due. Never mind, they can all fuck themselves. He'll make sure he gets Respect.

FEAR IS THE KEY

'It's not catastrophes, murders, deaths, diseases that age and kill us,' wrote Virginia Woolf, 'it's the way people look and laugh, and run up the stairs of omnibuses.'

As any old-school comedian would tell you, she didn't play the Glasgow Empire on a Saturday night. But she had a point. For most of us, everyday interactions with strangers determine the quality of our lives more than we care to admit. God knows what lethal traumas Virginia would have suffered if, as she took her seat on the train from Richmond, she found herself having to pick her way through pairs of legs sprawled over the seats, incessant ring tones, almost theatrical public profanity, and acres of ugly bare flesh. She might have put it down to the vulgarity of her despised hoi polloi. But what would undoubtedly have come as a shock to her would be the way in which a quiet fear ruled the reactions of the other passengers around her.

Most of us, thankfully, still have relatively little direct experience of violent crime, but the fact is that all but the most sheltered now suffer death by a thousand anti-social cuts: by the petty rudeness; the incivility that flies beneath the radar of criminality and ASBOs, but manages to utterly alienate; the terrible tales related by others; the sheer ugliness that accosts us. The streets are now ruled by the unruly; the show is run by the show-offs.

During his speech outside 10 Downing Street on the morning after his third election victory, Tony Blair proclaimed his desire to foster a culture of 'respect', a line obviously inserted in response to the growing unease with the way in which all public places were apparently increasingly being dominated by the loud, the brutish and the downright violent. It was an unfortunate choice of word, for one reason alone: for those responsible for such behaviour, 'respect' equals 'fear'. Jason understands this.

In his book *Yob Nation*, Francis Gilbert wrote that, in his view:

> [A] yob is not like most criminals who wish to be secretive in what they do. Yobs like nothing more than to be seen and heard. Whereas a genuine 'gang member' will quietly threaten somebody with death if he does not do his bidding, a yob will publicly humiliate his chosen victim in the streets, calling for all his mates to have a look… [T]ime and time again when I interviewed yobs they all said that they loved watching the fear on people's faces as they stood around doing absolutely nothing.

Or, as he could have added, as they drove. Is there anybody who, if they are being completely honest, would dare ask a couple of young men in the next vehicle to turn down the booming thud of music that emanates from their car as it waits at the traffic lights? The point of such stereophonic displays of noise pollution is, on the one hand, to attract attention and, on the other, to repel people. It is now a feature of all high streets, and it has absolutely the desired effect: it is unsettling and threatening, and it dares you to protest. Anybody who has experienced it will be familiar with the mixture of responses it induces – contempt for the idiots inside their vibrating motor and the way in which they are imposing their will on you, coupled with a complete helplessness at having to accept it. They have done nothing to earn your respect, but much to make you fearful.

This is, of course, the way of the bully, and in a wider sense the compliant majority have ceded control to the bullying tendency. For example, on my journey home on the train to South East London, it is depressing to see how commuters now actively accommodate and work round those who impose themselves unthinkingly on what is a communal space, effectively taking it over and diminishing everybody else in the process. For such individuals, it is now *de rigueur* to stake out a space by putting their feet up on the seat opposite. This increasingly common and apparently victimless practice is, in fact, one that combines all the worst aspects of anti-social behaviour: it is utterly selfish in the context of a public place, it implies a complete disregard for fellow travellers, and a contempt for the person who will have to sit where dirty shoes have been.

In our new universe, if asked to remove his feet, it is the bully who looks utterly offended – insulted that he is being shown such disrespect. If he complies, he will, in his myopic view, look silly in the eyes of others. On a couple of occasions, I have tentatively asked for feet to be taken off the seat, only to be told how fucking rude I was, and asked who the fuck I thought I was. This was then followed by a mobile phone conversation, during which these points were made again, loudly, so that my humiliation could be further drawn out.

On neither occasion, I might add, did anyone else back me up. Those who have not fully got to grips with the extent of social breakdown would like to explain this lack of support by referring to a traditional British desire not to make a scene or create a fuss. It's a nice idea, but it no longer holds water: the other cheek is now turned out of fear rather than embarrassment. And justifiably so: verbal abuse is bad enough for most people, but there is a genuine threat of possible physical violence that they now have to take into account. Adult men have, after all, been kicked senseless for less. In August 2007, Roger Hare, a 62-year-old grandfather, was left in a coma and on a life-support system after having been battered and knocked out of a train carriage – for asking a 20-year-old man to move his feet. At the subsequent trial, the young man pleaded self-defence. Similarly, and around the same time, a London man died after being struck when he dared to remonstrate with two yobs who threw a half-eaten chocolate bar through his car window; and a young father was fatally attacked in Warrington when he confronted a group of thugs causing damage outside his home.

Onlookers in such situations feel unprotected, and are frozen into inaction. Whether it is intrusive dirty shoes on a train seat or, at the other end of the anti-social scale, a list of social plans being made at full volume on a mobile telephone, the only realistic course of action for most people at the moment is to endure it.

The same helplessness has characterised the way in which we have witnessed the growth of urban gang culture over an astonishingly short space of time. This has been a feature of American cities for a number of decades now, aided and abetted by the culture of posturing and violence ('Get Rich or Die Trying'), not to mention the misogyny and homophobia promoted in hip-hop lyrics, and the juvenile celebration of ostentatious displays of vulgarity and wealth – so-called 'Bling' – by black hip-hop 'artists'. Gangs rule their particular patches of territory by inspiring dread; while researching Los Angeles gang warfare, I was told that simply looking at a gang member in the 'wrong' way was sometimes a justification for murder. The extent to which this culture has taken root in British towns and cities became apparent in the summer of 2007, when Rhys Jones, an 11-year-old Liverpool boy, was killed – shot at point-blank range for no discernible reason. A similar fate befell the murdered black teenager Jessie James in London, although in that case the jumped-up self-appointed lords of the street had felt 'disrespected' by his refusal to join them.

There has been palpable shock among the public at the sheer number of gangs now known to be operating in major cities. Stifled tears from the new home secretary, Jacqui

Smith, and a request that guns should be handed in hardly inspired confidence; rather it confirmed in many the belief that any genuine political will to do anything about the situation had been lost.

QUEUE ANARCHY

In the context of gang killings and everyday intimidations, the fate of the humble queue – that silent expression of collective social cohesion in the public arena – seems small beer. But its gradual decline into extinction, especially in our large cities, is emblematic of this social fracture, and that is how most people experience it. Take a single trip through London by bus, and see how many orderly queues you can spot. They have mostly been replaced with motley gatherings round the bus stop, which turn into a free-for-all once the number 137 turns up. The crowd surges towards the doors, never mind who was there first, and heedless of the old or infirm. There's a resigned air when the doors close, and people retreat once again to the pavement to take their chance next time round.

Of course, there is no doubt that the huge increase in population has had an impact here: put enough rats in a cage and they will end up killing each other. But the disappearance of this particular piece of public behaviour, once almost a definition of Britishness, is due more to a cultural shift than to simple demographics. The very principle of queuing is anathema – not just to the bully, but also to those who have little concept of decent collective civic life, who are not alive to others, or who consider themselves too special to have to worry about such worthy niceties.

It never crosses Jason's mind to queue. He also might well have a case of ADD, so we should probably end it here and make his chapter nice and short.

CHAPTER SEVEN

MIRROR, MIRROR

Yes, we are all individuals!
(...I'm not)

Monty Python's *Life of Brian*

Are Kayleigh, Harriet, Marc & Sue and Jason the face of modern Britain? They would certainly appear to be the most visible part of it, which should make them happy. They are responsible, whether intentionally or not, for setting the current, degraded tone in our national life. In their different ways, they bend society to fit their vision of themselves, to influence it and make sure they are seen doing it by the rest of us. And they have proved remarkably successful. Among the rest of us – still, surely, the majority – there are few who are happy with that. Whether we like it or not, we are assailed daily by the media's coverage of nonentities whose thirst for fame outstrips everything else. And on an everyday basis we have to live with the self-absorption, self-importance, exhibitionism and selfish anti-social behaviour of others, without having much choice in the matter.

Some would argue that this is just the logical and fair conclusion stemming from a society that celebrates and promotes the individual. What, they would say, is so wrong with people expressing their self-belief, or wanting to stand out and be different or unique in some way? Isn't the theme of this book built on a pointless, possibly snobbish nostalgia for some mythical golden age of repressed emotion and stiff upper lips, when people knew their place, God ordered their estate, and all was right with the world?

Such questions miss the point entirely. A strong belief in the importance of the individual, and in personal responsibility and autonomy – which has always been valued in our society and which is one of the tenets of traditional conservative thought – is something that we should continue to protect at all costs. Few would seriously dispute now that economic dynamism, without which there would be no society, flows from the encouragement of individual initiative, endeavour and enterprise. Only the seriously deluded now argue against this in favour of the life-sapping, spirit-deadening (and regularly murderous) hand of socialism.

But there is nothing contradictory about an adherence to the principle and practice of individualism and a belief, too, in a bigger external entity – be it a family, a locality or a nation, or indeed a sense of collective identity. There is no country more capitalistic, more celebratory of personal belief, and more willing to give everybody a shot than the United States. It is the birthplace of modern celebrity. Aspiration is virtually a religion. And, of course, it has exported some of the more questionable methods of personal development. As we have seen, it also has its own problems with social fragmentation. Yet despite this, the social and cultural landscape there is incomparably less toxic than it is in Britain. A belief in the individual exists side by side with a collective sense of neighbourhood, and a strong belief in both an overarching national identity and a national story – something which so bemuses Europeans that it causes them to go into convulsions of hate.

What our cast of characters have illustrated in their various ways is something quite different – a culture adrift from its moorings, and a majority that is apparently unable or unwilling to resist the tyranny of the shallow, the show-off, the self-appointed spokesman, the brutish and the spoilt. It's hardly surprising that it is this atmosphere – just as much as high taxation and the impact of unparalleled immigration – that (sometimes at the unconscious level) causes increasing numbers of us to flee abroad. A record high of nearly 200,000 left for good in 2006 alone. Some of these will have opened their paper in the morning and despaired at yet more cover-age of bleating *Big Brother* morons; have had to shout to make themselves heard during a simple restaurant meal; have been confronted with one yob too many on a journey home; or have been told just once too often that they were provin-cial reactionaries for not accepting it all as part and parcel of a culture that is vibrant, cutting-edge, diverse, etc., etc., etc.

The cults of youth and celebrity, which we have looked at here, and the all-pervasive influence of the Me Generation, have, of course, had their effects across the whole of the West. *Hello!* is, after all, a Spanish magazine in origin; people go bowling alone in Cincinnati; and the Italian street life we so romanticise has succumbed to the babble and rabble of binge-drinking and even more mobile phone conversations than in Britain. And across Europe, the falling birth rate might well be down, in part, to the sheer, prohibitive expense of raising children, as well as to nihilism and a general gloom about the future; but it is also surely a by-product of individual self-centredness and self-absorption.

In her recent book, *No Kid*, the French writer Corrine Maier listed 40 reasons why a woman should not have chil-dren. Maier is obviously a *provocateuse*, having already riled her countrymen on the issue of their laziness, and so should, of course, be taken with a pinch of salt; but some of her reasons would be considered utterly valid by her intended readers. She blames the state's obsession with the family for the pressure to have children, and naturally, being a French middle-class writer, she blames capitalism; but also, as she said in a recent interview, kids are there to stop you enjoying yourself:

> It's a child's hidden face. Believe me, he will be very inventive in this area. He will be ill when you (finally) arrange a night out, he will bug you when you celebrate your birthday with your friends, he will hate it if you bring someone he's never met back for the night, and beyond that you won't dare tread for fear of traumatising him for life.

No woman should have to have children if she doesn't want them, and Maier is undoubtedly writing for effect; but still, this is noxious stuff.

So the broader trends referred to in this book are not just British phenomena. But it is here that the cultural change would appear, on the face of it, to have been most profound. How the British actually behave, and how they are traditionally perceived by other nationalities – indeed, how many of them still perceive themselves – would seem never to have been more at variance with one another. But before we consider the broader reasons for this, it might be useful to look first at a number of examples which could be advanced as evidence that the situation is not, in fact, as bleak as I may have painted it.

REASONS TO BE CHEERFUL?

'I can scarcely remember a time when I have been more proud of my adopted country', wrote the columnist Janet Daley in the *Daily Telegraph* recently:

> Just as we had become reconciled to the idea that our chief national pastimes were whingeing, vomiting in the streets and breaking into each other's cars, along came a series of real threats to life and property and – who would have thought it? – the British still can take it, and behave like troupers in the process.

She was talking about the reaction to the abortive terrorist incidents in London and Glasgow, and the floods that caused such damage across the country in the summer of 2007. It was, indeed, cheering to see local communities helping each other out in watery extremis without making a big song and dance about it. This certainly didn't seem to be a case of the kind of conspicuous compassion favoured by Kayleigh, Harriet or Marc & Sue, but a genuine collective response to the misfortune of neighbours and even strangers. There was little scope for theatrics; you would have been little help if all you could contribute was to stand round, head bowed, weeping.

It is encouraging to think that instances such as this are proof that we are not quite as atomised as all that. Is there not still a country out there which goes on much as before, out of the limelight, not just busy filling in its application for the *Big Brother* house? There are little pieces of evidence which, in their different ways, suggest this. I was prompted, a year or so ago, to start looking seriously into the themes of this book when I read, by chance, two quite random statistics. The first was that the Royal Horticultural Society now boasts around 370,000 members. The second was that membership of the National Trust hovers around a massive three million – making it one of the biggest voluntary organisations of its kind in the world.

For many of these people, gardening or heritage enthusiasts alike, being 'sad' surely still meant the opposite of being happy. More importantly, both of these figures suggested the existence of a country that had, by some odd process, completely fallen from view.

As Citizens of the World, Marc & Sue and their ilk find such pursuits at best very amusing, and at worst insufferably narrow; although, and despite the numbers involved, they can be written off as being the preoccupations of older, fuddy-duddy generations. It is likely, therefore, that they would have experienced actual physical pain at the sight of the huge crowds which gathered in the Mall in London to celebrate the Queen's Golden Jubilee in 2002.

Walking along the ceremonial route on that occasion, I was struck by a sense in which the people there – who were drawn this time from all age groups – were part of a country that was kept increasingly under lock and key by its metropolitan masters. Prior to the event, the tone of coverage had been that the forthcoming anniversary was going to be an embarrassing flop; that people no longer cared; that society had changed its priorities; and that the monarchy was simply no longer one of those priorities. Of course, it is true that one certainly does not have to be a monarchist to believe passionately in the need for national community and communal feeling. But there was no question that the outpouring of affection for a figure who otherwise had virtually nothing to do with the day-to-day lives of the people who came to cheer her was evidence of her importance to them as a symbol of something bigger than just themselves.

It took the self-appointed opinion-formers by surprise, knocking them off balance, which probably explains why, after the Jubilee, they fell on the Paul Burrell trial story with such glee. Explaining at the time why he felt that, despite this popular feeling, the monarchy's days were numbered, Theodore Dalrymple wrote that the intelligentsia had decided on it – and what it wanted, it usually got:

> If we can't get rid of the monarchy just yet, pleaded one columnist in the *Observer*, let's at least cut it down to size. This, of course, is a plea that will appeal to every malcontent with a university degree who believes that the System has failed to recognize his imperishable genius. The size to which the monarchy must be cut down is my size, the size of Me.

That same intelligentsia is undoubtedly somewhat disturbed by the extraordinary resurgence of the Cross of St George in the past decade, and by the increasing appearance (not necessarily during big matches) of the English flag on car bonnets and private houses. This has been the more overt sign of a general exploration of what it means to be English, and, it has to be said, of a self re-assignment by many of their nationality. Those who would once have considered themselves British are now calling themselves English. Perhaps because, for them, Britishness has become too nebulous a concept to have any real meaning. Whatever the reasons, displaying the flag is certainly more of a case of saying *Look at Us*, rather than *Look at Me*.

OUT WITH THE OLD, IN WITH THE ME

There will be some readers (like Marc & Sue) who will doubtless be thinking: 'Ah, now I know where you're going with this...Monarchy, England flags...this just amounts to another reactionary call to go back to the good old, bad old days!'

Not so. These examples are, however, worth quoting, simply because they offer illustrations of expressions of a collective identity that come from what one might call the grassroots. However, the important point here is that such expressions are no longer widely culturally encouraged – certainly not by the elites – and are therefore swimming against the tide. They are not part of the orthodoxy, and they could not count as being of great importance in the land when it comes to setting the tone of its culture. Those same readers might also ascribe many of the issues we have looked at in this book to the changes wrought by Thatcherism. To a great extent, this has become the received wisdom, at least among those who generally form our cultural agenda for us: that the Thatcher years unleashed an aggressive, greedy cult of individualism; that we are still paying the price for her supposed belief that there 'is no such thing as society'. It doesn't matter that, for once, the defence of words being 'taken out of context' is absolutely justified; the words have stuck, as proof of her malign intent (and have remained potent enough for the Tory leader, David Cameron, to distance himself from them as a matter of priority). Ostentatious hedonism, self-absorption, a hysterical obsession with celebrity, and yobbish bullying are all put forward by commentators, both here and in America, as signs of a decadence brought on by an excess of capitalism and its trading of people as commodities.

This is a neat little argument; however, just as it is utterly inadequate in explaining the extent of the changes in British society, so it fails to absolve the liberal elites from having to face up to the results of their handiwork. Certainly, there is a case for suggesting that, for example, the arrival in the past decade and a half of 24-hour commercial media hugely expanded the need for what TV producers call 'content', and that this must go some way to explaining the growth in numbers (if not in talent or glamour) of the 'personalities' who could be used to fill the acres and acres of new broadcast space. It is true, too, that the displays of conspicuous happiness indulged in by Harriet and her friends are, at least in part, an attempt to live up to the images of successful, 'happening' people that come at them from the magazines and TV shows they lap up. And, more broadly, it is also undeniable that the economic changes which took place in the last two decades of the 20th century – the decline in manufacturing industries, and the subsequent effects that had on a previously structured workforce – have had a considerable influence on the way in which people relate both to their work and, indeed, to the communities that surround them.

But the preoccupations, attitudes and behaviour we have looked at in previous chapters are the end result of changes that have taken decades to come to the boil. They are the product of a cultural approach that was there well before Thatcher's election victory in 1979, or the triumph of a supposedly unfettered capitalism.

The Right might well have won the economic battles; but large parts of it never really understood the culture war that was happening under its very nose throughout the post-war period. What started off as a counter-culture became the ruling orthodoxy; and, to a remarkable degree, it is still in place. With one or two exceptions, its effects have largely been destructive, and the air is thick with chickens coming home to roost.

It can certainly shoulder much of the blame for the way in which traditional identities have been repudiated. Its distaste, if not outright contempt, for the idea of the nation or a belief in national pride has become part of the collective psyche. This attitude is now so embedded that we no longer see it, taking it for granted as the natural way of looking at things. A vigorous satirical tradition is one thing; systematic self-denigration to the point of oblivion quite another. This might, in part, account for the uphill struggle Gordon Brown has had, despite his valiant efforts to ignite a discussion on what it means to be British.

Similarly, the undermining of the family was as much a philosophical as a fiscal process: the nuclear unit was portrayed as the source of much emotional and psychological trauma (and for Marxists, the basic component holding up the hated capitalist structure). And in education, despite growing mountains of evidence of its shocking failure, an egalitarian approach is still, remarkably, clung to by many in the profession, as is the mistaken belief, discussed in an earlier chapter, that learning should emanate from the omnipotent pupil himself.

Underlying these attitudes, and most importantly for our discussion, any form of restraint, either internal or external, came to be judged on principle as a Bad Thing. This belief, which has seen perhaps its most disastrous results in the junking of discipline in schools, is nothing less than a betrayal of subsequent generations. Individuals, it was said, should be encouraged to express themselves in any way they saw fit, regardless of the consequences and effects on others – or indeed on themselves (a close friend, a thorough-going product of the '68 generation, related with amusement how he and his friends would sit on the floor of a railway station, getting filthy in the process, because sitting on the seats provided would have been regarded as simply too 'establishment'). Self-restraint or self-discipline were seen as oppressive, old-fashioned, even anti-creative. (A simple exposure to the rigour with which real artists or entrepreneurs apply themselves to their work is all the proof required to show quite how big a lie this particular mantra was.) And authority – in whatever shape or form, be it uniformed or moral – was, naturally, there to be resisted and dismantled.

This went hand in hand with the dogmatic relativism that has crept into most corners of our public and personal lives. If there is no absolute and verifiable truth, then no view has any greater validity than any other. Paradoxically, the result of this is that all views and judgements are not lowered, but rather raised, to an equal level of importance. A doctor's medical expertise may take no precedence over the possibly ill-informed view and experience of his fractious patient. Parents can upbraid a teacher for trying to impose order on their disruptive child. My opinion is as good as yours, simply by virtue of the fact that I hold it; and if I have a louder voice, then maybe mine will prevail. Who are you to say that I am wrong? Who says that Lucian Freud is a greater painter than Jack Vettriano? So what that you're an art critic – my opinion is worth just as much as yours! Aren't we all entitled to our own judgement? I know I am a caring, compassionate person, because this is how I see myself. I know that Diana was murdered by the secret services, and despite all this evidence to the contrary that you've put before me, I *know* I'm right! And I know I have the X factor, *too!*

It is no wonder, then, that, according to a number of recent surveys, so many people feel a sense of unease and unhappiness amid the chaos. The wholesale degradation and discrediting of structures, institutions and traditional collective identities has left many in our society stranded. Like life-jacketed survivors of the *Titanic*, they bob around on the surface of the ocean, screaming as loud as they can to be heard above the others, desperate to be seen.

CHAPTER EIGHT

LOOKING AHEAD

We were much further out than you thought, and not
waving but drowning.

With apologies to Stevie Smith

And the band played on. The noisy, hyperactive, crowded
surface of our society is taken as proof by many that this is
a dynamic, glittering place. Study it a little longer and you
might conclude that actually noise, hyperactivity and
crowds are *all* there is. Go deeper still and another picture
might emerge – of a country bemused by what it has apparently become; uncomfortable with being in thrall to the
celebrity cult, the show-off and the bully, and yet powerless to
do anything about it. How do we stop the cacophony of the
band from drowning out the creaks and groans of a ship in
distress?

Sorely aware of the fracturing that has taken place, most
mainstream politicians now talk of the need for strong community, for a revived sense of civic pride and duty. Cameron's
Conservatives, in particular, highlight the important part to
be played by the private citizen in such collective efforts as
charitable, local and volunteer associations. Political spin-
doctoring, whereby the act of being seen to do something is
more important than the doing itself, no longer works, even
for those sophisticates who always saw through it but were
nevertheless fascinated by the game. Even the excessive image-
consciousness of the Blair governments has given way to a less
starry – not to say positively dour – tone. Whatever the later
disasters, in this respect it was almost refreshing to see

Gordon Brown, awkward and kitted out much as Harold Wilson might have been, on his summer break in the UK, with no celebrity villa or host in sight and, thank goodness, with no swivel-eyed spouse there to get in on the act.

There are other, albeit tiny, indications that exhaustion might be setting in. Audience ratings for *Big Brother* have declined, and Channel 4 has announced that there will be no Celebrity version in 2008. And Simon Cowell's biggest TV hit in 2007 was *Britain's Got Talent* – yet another audition show maybe, but oddly old-fashioned in that it generated a harmless, strange sense of patriotism, its main purpose being to find an act that would be good enough to join the line-up at the Royal Variety Performance.

The undignified, childish and self-serving behaviour of the servicemen and servicewomen held hostage by the Iranians gave even the most mawkish among the population, their candles at the ready, a severe and presumably frustrating jolt. And despite a tsunami of media coverage, the crowds that turned out for the 10th anniversary of the death of Diana, that *über*-celebrity of the western world, were decidedly thin.

Of course, there are some genies that, once out, prove impossible to stuff back into their bottles, however hard we might try. Gone forever, surely, is the extraordinary talent for understatement that once characterised this country. Whether in speech or behaviour, a quality of which we were undisputed masters, and which informed everything from the wording of wartime propaganda posters to the best in our wit and satire, has disappeared entirely. In this respect, Britain's past is not so much a different country as an alien universe. There can be no more George Sanderses, Noël Cowards or Joyce Grenfells. The power of understatement is simply no longer recognised; now we are slaves to the Totally Amazing and the Completely, Incredibly Bizarre.

Virtually extinct, too, is the real English eccentric. The genuine article simply cannot compete in a landscape full of people convinced of their own specialness, unique requirements and unconventionality. We still talk proudly of our particular way with street fashion, our own quirky, subversive style of dress. But in a high street full of pierced bare flesh, ostentatious bling and raw exhibitionism, this is an illusion. The true eccentric is now the individual happy to be ordinary and out of the limelight.

But if we really do believe that there is a bigger world than those inhabited by Kayleigh, Harriet, Marc & Sue and Jason, if we are genuinely concerned about the gradual disintegration of the public arena, and if we really do despair at the debasement of our culture, then it will require a fair amount of courage to do any more than just sit back and wait, in the complacent belief that society and fashion run in cycles which come to an end of their own accord. So, what to do?

THINK OUTSIDE THE BOX

Television could play a big part in lessening the current frenzied preoccupation with celebrity and the need to be visible at all costs, regardless of talent or deed. All it would require is some nerve on the part of producers and commissioning editors. At the moment, their reflex action is to reach for the celebrity guest, or to turn down any new idea that doesn't have a 'name' attached to it. This is a trend that has intensified in the past few years, to the point where programmes and formats that could happily exist in their own right – indeed that *have* existed as such in the past – without the addition of 'personalities' as either presenters or guests, do not get made. It is self-perpetuating, so it has become a pillar of TV wisdom that this is what the audience wants, expects and will not tune in without.

Whether this is actually true is highly questionable. My own experience of making documentary profiles tended to show that, more often that not, the name of the subject made little real difference to the ratings. Of course, certain stars will always act as a draw; but these are actually very few in number. Executives and programme makers seem to be in the grip of a group-think, the like of which is more usually associated with the movie industry, where faith in the all-important pulling-power of famous actors is largely unquestioned by the studios. Time and again, the weekend box-office figures tell Hollywood that it is the subject matter, the story or the genre that gets people into the cinemas, and that even a star of the magnitude of Tom Cruise cannot attract punters to something that does not appeal to them. Yet still, lacking the confidence to make a judgement, or simply misreading the reasons for a film's success, they hanker after a name. Television operates along increasingly similar lines. Yet television has it within its power to change.

The current approach reinforces the impression, at least among impressionable types like Kayleigh, that to be one of these celebrities is to own the key to existence. Reality shows might be full of freaks, but they offer the self-promoter and the vacant show-off a route onto the daytime sofa, and then, if they're lucky, maybe their own game or chat show. This bandwagon could be slowed down without much trouble if, quite simply, broadcasters made the decision to embark on a little experiment and to give the whole celebrity circus a rest – deny it the oxygen of publicity for a while. They would then have to be imaginative. But they might find themselves pleas- antly surprised by the results. They might also help restore some value to fame's badly eroded currency. And, in punch- ing a hole in the wall of white noise that comes at us every week, they would also be doing our culture a real service.

REDISCOVER THE ADULT WITHIN

On the other hand, any attempt to reverse the Me-fixated infantilisation of society would require a Herculean effort. The prospects of an overhaul of the education system, in which children could once again learn adulthood and reach their true potential through self-discipline, structure and the imposition of an unapologetic authority, are at best extremely remote; and even if such a change were proposed, it is likely that it would be unworkable within our current legal frame- work, and be undermined by unco-operative, egotistical parents.

Still, voices on all sides are increasingly being raised about the inadequacy of the state system – not least among those who could usually be relied upon to rally to its defence. The left-wing Institute for Public Policy Research (IPPR) recently published a report, which recommended that such traditional public school institutions as the house system and cadet force be reintroduced to the state sector, to help working-class children acquire the kind of interactive personal and social skills that might help narrow the gap between rich and poor.

'We have looked hard at the evidence, and children do better in these conditions', said Richard Darlington of the IPPR in *The Times*. 'We have to challenge some of the hippy tendencies of the Left on youth activities. Actually what works is structure, discipline, uniform and hierarchy.'

Sir Bufton Tufton couldn't have put it better.

When it comes to the posturing of the bully, the anti-social element and the yob, those from quite different political traditions sense that society is spiralling out of control. Over the past couple of years, conversation after conversation has left me convinced that Disgusted no longer resides just in Tunbridge Wells, but around the dinner tables of Islington, Highbury and even Hampstead. Perhaps the results of what were, for people like Marc & Sue, nice ideas on paper are finally confronting them via a brick through the sash window.

Rather than waiting for long-term tinkering to bear fruit, it is perhaps becoming increasingly clear to more and more people that a radical course of action is needed if the wheels are not to come off altogether. Declaring 'Bring back National Service!' is a shortcut way to getting a good laugh, and many who might secretly believe that *well...it did have its advantages* would choke if asked seriously to publicly champion it now. Besides, the military, we are told, wouldn't wear it. But it is evidence of the drift of much thinking on this subject that consideration is being given to some sort of national programme aimed at young people.

In a speech a couple of years ago, David Cameron described how he wanted to create a 'new National Movement', which would reproduce in school leavers the sense of shared achievement experienced by people of his father's generation who did National Service. He was not talking about bringing it back – he is a moderniser, after all – but he did want young people to have the same feeling of having achieved 'something we all did together'. His instinct, he said, was that it should be compulsory:

> If it isn't compulsory, or if it isn't universal, it could tend to be something else that well-off families do because it's good for their kids, but it would not actually reach some of the most marginalised families and excluded children who actually would really benefit.

The scheme could, he said, range from building hospitals in Rwanda to helping with social services in Stepney:

> We should view this new enterprise as something for every young person in our country. An essential part of growing up to be a British citizen, not just an add-on extra for a select few.

This was certainly going in the right direction. Unfortunately, details of the proposal, when they were finally announced in 2007, indicated a much more modest, watered-down plan, consisting of a non-compulsory six-week period, as opposed to the three or four months originally envisaged by Cameron.

This was a pity. A voluntary scheme would make next to no difference – Cameron's initial instinct was the right one. Six weeks – indeed even three or four months – would also prove wholly inadequate in effecting any lasting change. A year would, instead, have sent out the message that what was being undertaken was considered by the country to be of vital importance – that, in other words, we meant business.

Similarly, building hospitals in Rwanda might be taken out of the equation. This is not out of any distaste for foreign aid, but rather because this is the sort of project that is currently undertaken by students in the now seemingly universal 'gap' year (up to 200,000 people annually take a 'year out', including 130,000 school leavers), and that is all too often regarded by them as simply a means of exploring their own personal development and growth. In fact, the Voluntary Service Overseas (VSO) charity recently said that such 'voluntourism' was often badly planned and was more concerned with satisfying the demands of the students than the requirements of the local communities.

It is probably true to say that many of these students, hyper-sensitive as they are about their own self-evolvement, would shudder at the suggestion that they might help out those nasty chavs closer to home. That's if the thought has ever crossed their minds; for your average Citizen of the World, Nuneaton will always lose out to Namibia. A strictly domestic national scheme, which would increase the participants' already sadly depleted stock of knowledge about their own society, is just what is needed. A Citizen of the World can, after all, so easily be a Citizen of Nowhere.

ANSWER BACK

The people who fought World War II – characterised by the American journalist and anchorman Tom Brokaw as 'the greatest generation' – did not make great claims, and would not have baulked at being considered ordinary. It would not have occurred to them that there was anything wrong with the label. However, measured against the yardsticks we are accustomed to using today, they were anything *but* ordinary.

It should be all about Us, not just all about Me. After 9/11, there was much talk of society putting away its childish things – the time had come to get serious. That turned out to be spurious. We may well have to wait longer for many of us to realise that a fascination with ourselves will only take us so far, and that it will, ultimately, prove deeply unsatisfying, as well as destructive and divisive.

In the meantime, we can, to borrow a phrase much favoured by anarchist groups, reclaim the streets – or at least make a start.

We can throw dignity to the wind and shout back at Kayleigh that no, we're not jealous of her white limo. We can summon up all our patience and explain to Harriet that yes, we do indeed have a life, but that maybe she could just be a bit quieter in proclaiming what is, actually, her lack of one. We can shock Marc & Sue by expressing an irony-free enthusiasm for something conventional. And those brave souls among us can ask Jason to remove his feet from the seat.

As we have seen, there's a real danger of serious abuse here. But, as they used to say, if enough of us do it...